The Pelican Guide to

OLD HOMES OF MISSISSIPPI

VOL. 1: Natchez and the South

By
HELEN KERR KEMPE

Edited by
Susan Cole Doré

PELICAN PUBLISHING COMPANY
GRETNA 1989

First edition, March 1977
Second printing, January 1979
Second edition, September 1989

Library of Congress Cataloging-in-Publication Data

Kempe, Helen Kerr.
    The Pelican guide to old homes of Mississippi / by Helen
Kerr Kempe ; edited by Susan Cole Doré. — 2nd ed.
        p. cm.
    Includes index.
    Contents: v. 1. Natchez and the South.
    ISBN 0-88289-750-0 (v. 1)
    1. Historic buildings—Mississippi—Guide-books. 2.
Mississippi—Description and travel—1981- —Guide-books.
3. Dwellings—Mississippi—Guide-books. 4. Architecture,
Domestic—Mississippi—Guide-books. I. Doré, Susan Cole.
II. Title. III. Title: Old Homes of Mississippi.
F342.K45 1989
917.6204'63—dc20   89-8488
                                                             CIP

Information in this guidebook is based on authoritative data available at the time of printing. Hours of operation of establishments listed are subject to change without notice. Readers are asked to take this into account when consulting this guide.

Manufactured in the United States of America

Published by Pelican Publishing Company, Inc.
1101 Monroe Street, Gretna, Louisiana 70053

Contents

DOWNTOWN NATCHEZ

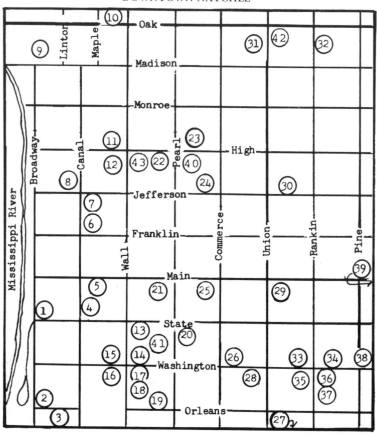

1. Evans-Bontura
2. The Parsonage
3. Rosalie
4. Banker's House
5. Commercial Bank
6. Priest's House and
   Lawyer's Lodge
7. The House on Ellicott's Hill
8. Villa Lombardo
9. Clifton Site
10. The Wigwam
11. Cherokee
12. Choctaw
13. Governor Holmes House
14. Dixie
15. Texada
16. Holly Hedges
17. Leisure House
18. Coyle House
19. Pleasant Hill
20. First Presbyterian Church
21. Mississippi Bank

22. Myrtle Terrace
23. Stanton Hall
24. Chamber of Commerce
25. Britton & Koontz Bank
26. Trinity Episcopal Church
27. Ravenna
28. Van Court Townhouse
29. St. Mary's Cathedral
30. King's Tavern
31. The Burn
32. Melmont
33. Peter Buttross House
34. Barnes House
35. Elward
36. Green Leaves
37. Presbyterian Manse
38. The Elms
39. Williamsburg
40. Dr. Dubs' Townhouse
41. Magnolia Hall
42. Shields Town House
43. William Harris House

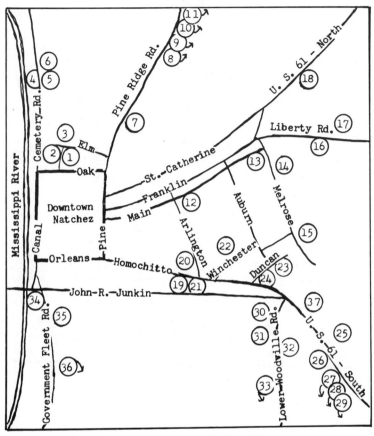

1 The Towers
2. Cottage Gardens
3. Airlie
4. Weymouth Hall
5. Natchez Cemetery
6. The Gardens
7. Concord Site
8. Edgewood
9. Lansdowne
10. Mistletoe
11. Mount Repose
12. Arlington
13. Monmouth
14. Linden
15. Melrose
16. Montaigne
17. Oakland
18. D'Evereux
19. Belvidere

20. Twin Oaks
21. Dunleith
22. Routhland
23. Auburn
24. Hope Farm
25. Glenwood Site
26. Elmscourt
27. Elgin Plantation
28. Cherry Grove
29. Fair Oaks
30. Hawthorne
31. Longwood
32. Gloucester
33. Saragossa
34. The Briars
35. Richmond
36. Glenfield
37. Glenburnie

Acknowledgments

I would like to thank the many individuals, organizations, and pilgrimage committees who provided me information about the homes and landmarks in this guide. Without their help, this book could not have been compiled.

Photography acknowledgments: Travel/Tourism Department of the Mississippi Agricultural and Industrial Board, Jackson; Pilgrimage Garden Club, Natchez; Port Gibson-Claiborne County Chamber of Commerce, Port Gibson; Windsor Ruins by S. Gaillard, photographer; Woodville Civic Club, Inc., Woodville.

Several individuals made great contributions to the preparation of the second edition. Thanks should go to Ernesto Caldeira of Rosemont plantation, Woodville; Anne Vaughan, Natchez Pilgrimage Tours; Judith Scruggs, Port Gibson-Claiborne County Chamber of Commerce; and Benita Dillard, Vicksburg Convention and Visitors Bureau.

The Pelican Guide to

OLD HOMES
OF MISSISSIPPI

VOL. 1: Natchez and the South

Entries designated by a 🏛 symbol are listed on the National Register of Historic Places.

Woodville Area

Introduction

This charming southwest Mississippi town, the county seat of Wilkinson County, has been described at Harvard University as the Southern town best typifying and preserving the traditions of the antebellum South. It was first settled in the 1700s and incorporated as a town in the Mississippi Territory in 1811. The original Natchez Trace had its point of origin at Fort Adams on the Mississippi River near Woodville.

Many Woodville area homes are open to group tours by appointment through the Woodville Civic Club, Box 814, Woodville, Mississippi 39669.

Argue Home

One of the earliest homes built in Woodville is the ARGUE HOME. The beautiful columned portico with an attractive doorway typifies the architectural influence of the Federal period. Private.

Church Street at College Street in Woodville.

Bowling Green Plantation

BOWLING GREEN, the setting of Stark Young's famous novel, *So Red the Rose,* was once the vast estate of the nationally prominent judge Edward McGehee. The mansion was burned by Northern troops in October 1864, and today all that remains on the grounds are three brick pillars, the carriage house, and the family cemetery.

The property remains in the hands of the McGehee family. Private. Group tours by appointment; contact the Woodville Civic Club.

Jackson Road, two miles east of U.S. 61, in Woodville.

Bramlette Law Office and Commercial Row

The small brick building at the east end of Commercial Row in Woodville is the BRAMLETTE LAW OFFICE. Built in the late 1800s by Captain D. C. Bramlette, a lawyer, it has been used by four generations of Bramlette attorneys. Commercial Row has been an integral part of the business community for more than a century.

South side of Courthouse Square in Woodville.

Catchings Home

Built in 1819, this imposing white, two-story house, also known as the A. M. Feltus home, was designed along the typical lines of the architecture of pre-Civil War days.

Four large columns support the roof and the front portico, which has an attractive fanlight entrance and upper balcony.

Private. Group tours by appointment; contact the Woodville Civic Club.

Corner First Street South and Depot Street in Woodville.

Day Home

This large white, one-and-a-half-story frame home was built by Confederate general Carnot Posey in 1845. Wood railings of the wide veranda and the fireplace mantels, which the general brought from an earlier home, are interesting features of this well-preserved cottage.

Private. Group tours by appointment; contact the Woodville Civic Club.

Church Street at Second Street South in Woodville.

Elsinore

Although not an old home, stately ELSINORE, a large two-story red brick colonnaded mansion, epitomizes all the charm and grandeur of Southern colonial architecture. Private.

U.S. 61 North, near the intersection with Prentiss Highway in Woodville.

Ferguson Home

John W. Goddard, a carpenter and undertaker in Woodville before the Civil War, built this attractive one-and-a-half-story cottage for his home.

Evidence of his craftsmanship may be noted in the solid walnut doors and mantels. The house has been carefully preserved by the present owners.

Private. Group tours by appointment; contact the Woodville Civic Club.

Main Street in Woodville.

Foster Home

This house, formerly the Van Eaton home, was built in two sections, the first to the right of the center hallway, in 1820. The addition to the left was incorporated into the design with perfect symmetry in the 1840s to make the cottage, with its sloping roof extending over the wide veranda, a lovely home.

Foster Home

A portrait of Governor Henry Johnson of Louisiana hangs in the dining room. A collection of furnishings from the Johnson and Stockett families, prominent in Woodville history, may be seen.

Private. Group tours by appointment; contact the Woodville Civic Club.

Church Street at Third Street South in Woodville.

Hampton Hall

HAMPTON HALL, in a parklike setting, was built in 1832. It is a two-story colonial home with four columns and double galleries framing the entrance, which features a beautiful fanlight doorway.

One of the largest homes in Woodville, it has been the residence of many prominent families and was carefully restored in 1946. A private cemetery is just north of the house.

Private. Group tours by appointment; contact the Woodville Civic Club.

U.S. 61 South, near the intersection with Depot Street in Woodville.

Hampton Hall

Lewis Home

This handsome, two-story red brick home has an imposing entrance with double galleries and a fanlight doorway. Built in 1832 by Governor Abram Scott, it is a fine example of Southern colonial architecture.

The descendants of John S. Lewis, who acquired the property in 1836, still maintain the house. Private.

Church Street at Third Street South in Woodville.

Magruder-Scott Home

A large two-and-a-half-story white house with broad double galleries, the MAGRUDER-SCOTT HOME was built in 1809. Restored in the 1870s by Dr. L. W. Magruder, Sr., it is still the residence of his descendants.

Private. Group tours by appointment; contact the Woodville Civic Club.

Second Street South at Natchez Street in Woodville.

Magruder-Scott Home

Methodist Church

Erected in 1824, this structure is the oldest Methodist church building in the state of Mississippi. Visitors welcome.

Main Street at Sligo Street in Woodville.

Railroad Office Building

The oldest railroad office building in the United States was built in Woodville in 1831, as headquarters for the pioneer Woodville-West Feliciana Railroad Company, which ran between Woodville and St. Francisville, Louisiana.

It is a handsome, classic twelve-pillared Greek Revival structure and has been used as a bank, a post office, and an office building. It will be the future home of the Woodville Museum of Southern Decorative Arts. The building is owned by the Woodville Civic Club, and is being restored.

East side of Courthouse Square in Woodville.

Railroad Office Building

Rosemont

Near Woodville is ROSEMONT plantation, a one-and-a-half-story home, painted brown and white, trimmed in green. This Mississippi planter's cottage has been restored with no structural change and with every aspect of its historical value preserved.

Huge wood-grained doors, at each end of the broad center hall, open to both front and back galleries to provide cooling airflow throughout the house.

Built between 1810 and 1814 by Samuel and Jane Cook Davis, parents of Jefferson Davis, only president of the Confederacy, the house remained the family home until 1895. Jefferson, one of ten children, was two years old when the family moved from Kentucky to Mississippi.

Jane Davis's spinning wheel still sits in the back room. Carefully preserved near the top of the stairs are the scrawled writings of her grandchildren. The rosebushes she planted and tended so many years ago still bloom. The family cemetery, containing the remains of five generations of the Davis family, may be seen on the grounds.

Rosemont

Jefferson Davis's boyhood home will give the visitor a look back into the nineteenth century.

Open to the public, Monday-Saturday, 10-4; nominal entrance fee.

One mile east of Woodville on Mississippi 24. 🏛

St. Paul's Episcopal Church

ST. PAUL'S is the oldest Episcopal church west of the Allegheny Mountains, dating from the 1820s. An important feature is the church organ, imported from England in 1827, a gift from A. M. Feltus. The rectory, just north of the church, is a typical early nineteenth-century Mississippi cottage. Visitors welcome.

Church Street at First Street South in Woodville.

Territorial Bank Building

This structure was built before 1817 as a branch of the Bank of the Territory of Mississippi. Steeped in the tradition and heritage of the Old South, the building is owned and is being restored by the Woodville Civic Club. Visitors welcome.

West side of Courthouse Square in Woodville.

Woodville Baptist Church

The sturdy red brick WOODVILLE BAPTIST CHURCH is the oldest building of any church denomination now standing in the state of Mississippi, dating from the early 1800s. The congregation was organized in 1798. The beautiful stained-glass window is a recent addition. Visitors welcome.

Natchez Street at First Street South in Woodville.

Woodville Baptist Church

Woodville Republican

The *Woodville Republican*, founded in 1824, has the distinction of being the oldest newspaper and the oldest business institution in the state of Mississippi. It was bought by Captain John S. Lewis in the mid-nineteenth century. His grandson, John S. Lewis, is editor emeritus of the paper, and his great-grandson, Andrew Jackson Lewis, is editor. Visitors welcome.

Depot Street at Second Street South in Woodville.

Cold Spring

The two-story colonial home, COLD SPRING, was built in the early 1800s by Dr. Carmichael. Four large columns support the spacious double galleries. It has remained in the McGehee Reed family for many generations.

Private. Group tours by appointment; contact the Woodville Civic Club.

In Pinckneyville.

Cold Spring

Desert Plantation

The one-and-a-half-story comfortable, sturdy cottage on DESERT PLANTATION depicts the illustrious history of prominent early settlers in Pinckneyville.

It was built about 1810 by Captain Semple. Except for a brief period, it has been the residence of the Merwin and Brandon families for many generations. The nearby cemetery has markers dating from 1813.

Visitors may see beautiful family furnishings and portraits of Gerard Brandon, first native-born governor of Mississippi, and his brother, General William Lindsay Brandon in full military dress.

Private. Group tours by appointment; contact the Woodville Civic Club.

In Pinckneyville.

Greenwood

Imposing GREENWOOD, a large two-story plantation home, was built in 1792 by Patrick Foley from Ireland. Members of the Foley and Keary families were its earliest occupants.

Since that time it has been the residence of Matthew Brandon, brother of Governor Gerard Brandon, also Henry Wall, John Nathaniel Evans, other Brandon and Evans families, and the Alvin P. Bedgoods, who have carefully restored it.

The furnishings include many beautiful French, English, and colonial pieces, some made to order in Europe, others handcrafted by slaves and resident carpenters.

Private. Group tours by appointment; contact the Woodville Civic Club.

In Pinckneyville.

Salisbury

This fine old country home is in a state of disrepair. It is a one-and-a-half-story house with six large columns supporting the roof that extends over a wide veranda. The drawing room is featured in the Louisiana State University Anglo-American Museum in Baton Rouge. The house has been in the possession of the Shepherd family since 1903, at which time it was reputed to be more than one hundred years old. Private.

Near Pond community.

John Wall House

Located near the Pond community is the JOHN WALL HOUSE, reported to be the oldest house in the state of Mississippi. John Wall acquired the property by Spanish land grant in 1794, and the primitive lines of the house attest to its age. It is an English raised cottage, built before 1760. Downstairs the walls are brick; upstairs they are brick laid between structural timbers.

In very poor condition, some preservation efforts have been made, and it is hoped that plans for restoration may be realized. Private.

One mile east of Pond community.

Fort Adams

This little community, established as a mission in 1682 by Father Davion, is the oldest settlement in Wilkinson County. It later became a U.S. frontier fort in 1799 under the command of Brigadier General James Wilkinson, for whom the county was named.

The fort site is on private grounds on the south edge of present-day FORT ADAMS. At the time of occupancy, there were extensive buildings, including a watchtower situated on a summit of the bluff overlooking the Mississippi River. In 1960 archaeologists from the Smithsonian Institution were able to verify the extent of the structures at the location.

The fort was the setting for Edward Everett Hale's story, *The Man Without a Country,* published in 1863.

Eighteen miles west of Woodville on Mississippi 24. 🏛

Indian Fields

This impressive Italianate house was built in approximately 1908. The house, outbuildings, and surrounding gardens have been restored. Private.

On Mississippi 24, west of Woodville.

Pleasant Hill

This distinguished example of a typical plantation residence has been sensitively restored and preserved. Private.

On Mississippi 24, east of Woodville. 🏛

Shamrock Plantation

Known for many years as Forrest Home Plantation or the Burton place, this imposing two-and-a-half-story double-galleried Southern plantation home dates from the 1830s.

The interior of the house, of South Carolina design, has the typical broad central hallways flanked by four large rooms on both levels.

SHAMROCK has remained a working plantation through a succession of owners, having made the transition from cotton to lumber to cattle.

Private. Group tours by appointment; contact the Woodville Civic Club.

Whitestown Road, eleven miles from Woodville.

Trinity Plantation

Built about 1860, TRINITY was moved during the nineteenth century to its present location from its original site nearer Fort Adams. Private.

On Mississippi 24, west of Woodville.

Holly Grove

This attractive home was built in the early 1790s by Duncan Stewart, first lieutenant governor of Mississippi (1817). The spacious double galleries with six massive columns and other additions were made in the 1830s.

The interior includes nine fireplaces, intricate Federal millwork, and beautiful furnishings.

Private. Group tours by appointment; contact the Woodville Civic Club.

In Centreville, near Woodville.

Rose Hall

A classic example of mid-Victorian architecture is ROSE HALL, built in 1899 for Lea Borden Robinson and his wife and ten children. The home is still occupied by his descendants.

The interior of this handsome two-story residence features a cellar and six large bedrooms. It was remodeled in 1940 and 1964.

Private. Group tours by appointment; contact the Woodville Civic Club.

St. Mary Street in Centreville, near Woodville.

Amite County Courthouse

The AMITE COUNTY COURTHOUSE is situated on the town square of Liberty. At one time Liberty served as a major crossroads of the Natchez-Mobile route—the road south leading to Bayou Sara, Louisiana, a thriving river town.

Much of the activity of the Civil War occurred at this location. The Amite Rifles and the Liberty Guards mustered here. It is reported, although not documented, that the building served as headquarters for both Union and Confederate troops.

The original design of the building, completed in May 1841, was a gabled-roof, two-story structure measuring fifty-four by forty square feet. Alterations were made in the 1930s by the WPA. Other additions have been made through the years to this diminutive, historic seat of Amite County government.

Main Street in Liberty. 🏛

Thomas Batchelor House

Soon after the Louisiana Purchase in 1803, settlers came to southwest Mississippi—among them George Gayden, whose daughter married Thomas Batchelor. Little is known of his early life, but Batchelor later became one of the leading landowners and successful planters in the area. In 1817, he served as a delegate to the constitutional convention that met in Washington, Mississippi, to lay the foundation for statehood.

His estate, Beech Grove, was a working plantation, and his home, built in the 1820s, was a sturdy, one-and-a-half-story raised cottage with a large veranda and dormered roof, which has served as the family residence for many generations. The home was carefully restored in 1959. Private.

Route 5, Olio Road in Liberty. 🏛

Little Red Schoolhouse

A remainder of bygone days is the LITTLE RED SCHOOL-HOUSE in Liberty, built in the 1800s. Until recently, it was the state's oldest school building in continuous use.

In Liberty.

Whitworth College

This educational institution has played an important role in higher education in the state of Mississippi since before the Civil War. It served as a Confederate college from 1861 to 1865.

A building used as a Confederate hospital has been torn down and replaced with a modern dormitory. The oldest buildings still standing on campus are Margaret Hall, built in 1878, and Johnson Hall, 1883.

In Brookhaven. 🏛

Natchez Area

Introduction

On a bluff overlooking the Mississippi River is Natchez, founded in 1714. This charming city, unrivaled in the number of antebellum homes within a close radius, has aged in a splendid manner. The years are becoming to her, and the local residents, many of whom are descendants of original property owners, continually restore and replenish the homes and gardens, affording the visitor a glimpse of the glory and romance of bygone days.

The architecture in Natchez reached a state of perfection during the mid-nineteenth century. The fall of cotton empires and the demise of steamboating on the river in no way deterred the citizens from preserving the classic beauty of their city.

The homes—mansion and cottage alike—have stood the test of time. In part this can be attributed to their construction, from handcut native cypress and pine carved from the surrounding virgin forests. The lumber was seasoned for years before it was acceptable, and it is in the nature of wood to harden with age. Plantation homes were built with an eye to comfort and necessity, with thick walls, high ceilings, and large rooms. All were planned with broad airways and wide galleries. It has been said that the difference between Southern plantation airways and galleries and ordinary halls and porches is as great as that between ocean liners and canoes.

Hospitality here, developed during this golden era which came to an abrupt halt in 1861, was unsurpassed in the nation. Food was plentiful and the comfortable homes could accommodate guests for days, even weeks. A man's home was really his castle; it was the crowning point of his life's work. Some of the planters would try to outdo others in the size and elaborate appointments of their new

uld build homes nearby for their children, ex-
heir who would carry on in his father's house—
the landed gentry.

nt toward sparing expense, beautiful and rare art
rniture were brought from Europe, New York,
New Orleans, and many of the items are in the
tings for which they were originally purchased.

In modern times it would be virtually impossible to reproduce these lovely homes. By today's standards the "cottage," often a home of ten or more rooms, would by no means be considered a small house. It is said that even in the humblest of Natchez homes there is something of the grand manner, and in the greatest mansion there is pure and simple elegance.

Several of the homes are open to the public year-round except during the spring and fall pilgrimages, when a pilgrimage ticket is required for entrance. Other Natchez homes are open only through Natchez Pilgrimage Tours, P.O. Box 347, Natchez, Mississippi 39121. Call (601) 446-6631; out-of-state, (800) 647-6742.

Many of these historic houses operate bed-and-breakfast facilities. Reservations for accommodations in most of these homes must be made through Natchez Pilgrimage Tours. Telephone numbers to call are listed at the end of each entry.

Airlie

The descendants of Ayres P. Merrill occupy AIRLIE, which dates back to the late 1700s. Some believe it to be the first residence built in the Natchez Territory.

A rambling cottage with a wide veranda, it stands twelve rooms broad as a result of several additions. The original central portion, like many other older houses in the area, is predominantly Spanish provincial, with beams and timbers held together by wooden pegs.

It is often referred to as the old Buckner home for the family who occupied it during the time of its first recorded history.

Clearly visible on the floor and walls of AIRLIE are the stains of blood shed during the Civil War.

The treasures in the home include rosewood and mahogany antique furniture, silver, and exquisite Du Barry china; also a portrait of "Sir" William Dunbar, an important landowner in the 1700s. Private.

Elm Street at the end of Myrtle Avenue in Natchez.

Arlington

ARLINGTON is situated in a peaceful setting surrounded by giant magnolias, moss-draped oaks, and Southern plantings. It is a two-story red brick Southern colonial mansion with a double portico, a beautiful fanlight entrance, and four stately white columns.

Completed in 1820, the home was built by Pierre Surget, one of the earliest settlers of Natchez, for his oldest daughter, Mrs. Jane White, who died suddenly on the first night in residence in her dream home. At her death, ARLINGTON and all its furnishings were left to her sister, Mrs. Bingaman. Five generations of the Surget family occupied the home and added to its wealth of treasures.

Arlington

ARLINGTON contains beautiful museum pieces and rare paintings. The gold drawing room with priceless objets d'art, a spinet piano more than three hundred years old, and a library housing several thousand books are representative of the contents of this elegant mansion. Private.

Main Street at Fourth Street in Natchez. 🏛

Auburn

In the early 1800s, Lyman Harding built AUBURN on acreage surrounded by natural beauty. It is a magnificent red brick structure with great white columns. Inside are spacious drawing rooms, dining rooms, a library, six huge bedrooms, and other smaller rooms.

The architectural details of the interior include handcarved doorways, fanlights, exquisite arches, moldings, cornices, and mantels. The feature attraction is a perfect spiral stairway that has been called "an architect's dream of beauty."

Dr. Stephen Duncan, one of Mississippi's first bankers, later acquired the home and property, which was presented to the city of Natchez by his descendants. It is located in Duncan Park and remains today in the same natural surroundings, which are ablaze with color in the spring when the dogwood and azaleas are in bloom.

Open to the public Monday-Saturday, 9-5; Sunday, 1:30-5. Call (601) 442-5981. Nominal entrance fee.

Corner of Duncan and Arlington streets in Natchez. 🏛

Banker's House

This two-story beige stucco house is connected by a common wall to the First Church of Christ Scientist, formerly the Commercial Bank.

It is a fine example of Greek Revival architecture built in about 1838 to house the treasurer of the bank, the two buildings being

Banker's House

connected for security reasons. The exterior features attractive Doric columns supporting the small entrance porch. Private.

107 South Canal in Natchez. 🏛

Barnes Home

This attractive home, beautifully preserved, was built in the 1830s on part of a 1795 land grant to William Barland.

The original house, two rooms downstairs and two upstairs, was one of three prefabricated houses shipped downriver from Ohio. The hardware in the main section bears the label of L. Fitzpatrick, the early Natchez foundryman who forged the first Bowie knife.

In the 1880s the dining room and kitchen were built. Other additions, including a kitchen with brick floors, exposed beams, and Douglas fir cabinets, complete this lovely home in a beautiful garden setting.

The color of the exterior is light mustard with black shutters, a combination used often in 1790 Delaware houses and eighteenth-century Williamsburg. Private.

705 Washington in Natchez.

Belvidere

Christopher Miller, secretary to the Spanish governor of Natchez, Gayoso de Lemos, was the builder of this simple white frame cottage, which originally was in the center of fourteen acres of wooded land, and later moved to its present location.

It has remained in the Kelly family for many generations with much of the original furniture, exquisite porcelain, and Venetian glass collection. Of special interest are two pictures, which are silhouettes of Samuel Brooks, the first mayor of Natchez, and his wife. Private.

Homochitto near Arlington Avenue in Natchez.

The Briars

THE BRIARS is a typical story-and-a-half country home with a broad veranda across the entire front, quaint old dormer windows, and many doors and large windows through which all the breezes can flow.

Built in 1812 by William Burr Howell, cousin of Aaron Burr, for Howell's wife, Louise Kempe Howell, it is of historical as well as architectural interest. In this home Varina Howell was born in May 1826, and was married to Jefferson Davis in February 1845.

It stands high on a bluff overlooking the river, secluded in deep woods, and was restored to its present beauty after it had fallen into a state of dilapidation for many years.

Today the serenity of THE BRIARS encompasses a historic shrine to Varina Howell Davis and her husband, Jefferson Davis, president of the Confederacy.

Overnight accommodations. Call (601) 446-9654; out-of-state, (800) 634-1818.

Access through Ramada Inn parking area in Natchez.

The Briars

Britton and Koontz First National Bank

The building now occupied by the bank is possibly the oldest in the South used in continuous service as a financial institution. Constructed in 1833, it is believed that it was originally the Agriculture Bank. Some alterations have been made, but the facade of this fine old building is of the original architectural design. At the time it was constructed it was described as "the finest banking building south of the Potomac River."

Prominent Natchez citizens associated with the BRITTON AND KOONTZ FIRST NATIONAL BANK include William Britton, George M. Koontz, Audley C. Britton, R. F. Learned, George W. Koontz, Melchior Beltzhoover, and A. B. Learned.

422 Main Street in Natchez.

Britton and Koontz First National Bank

The Burn

Built in the early 1830s by John P. Walworth, this homey-looking, story-and-a-half cottage has many spacious rooms, broad halls, mahogany woodwork, and hand-rubbed board floors.

THE BURN, named for the Scotch word for *brook* which ran by the property, is one of Natchez' antebellum homes that once was situated on vast acreage. This Greek Revival home has stood the test of time, fire, and war, and has been restored with strict observance of the original architecture.

Federal troops occupied the sturdy structure during the Civil War and today the name of a Major Coleman, cut by a diamond, is clearly visible in one of the windowpanes.

Open to the public daily, 9-5; nominal entrance fee. Call (601) 442-1344. Overnight accommodations. For reservations call (601) 446-6631; out-of-state, (800) 647-6742; ask for bed-and-breakfast department.

712 North Union in Natchez.

Peter Buttross Home

At one time known as the Wade House, this two-and-a-half-story white frame home, with a lacy wrought-iron fence, dates from the 1830s.

The architecture is typical of the large townhouses built during the golden era of Natchez and features a lovely stairway and beautiful furnishings. Private.

621 Washington in Natchez.

Cherokee

This imposing home, near the House on Ellicott's Hill, sits high on a knoll in the center of Natchez. Constructed in two sections, the original house, dating from 1794, was built by Jesse Greenfield on a Spanish land grant.

In 1810 the property was purchased by David Michie and the classic front, with recessed portico, was added, making

Cherokee

CHEROKEE one of the most attractive antebellum homes in Natchez. Private.

217 High Street at Wall Street in Natchez.

Cherry Grove

Pierre Surget, a native of New Rochelle, France, and a prominent early Natchez settler, built CHERRY GROVE for his wife, Katherine d'Hubert, in 1788 on land granted by Spain, which makes it one of Natchez' earliest residences.

A seaman for many years, Surget built the rambling home with the sturdiness of a seagoing vessel using handcut timbers and wooden pegs. The two-story house has the first story of brick and the second of frame, both of which have wide verandas. Access to the second level is by double winding stairways.

The home has remained in the Surget family since its construction, and Pierre and Katherine are buried in the family plot on the grounds. Private.

U.S. 61 (South), near Natchez.

Choctaw

This large three-level structure was built by the Neibert family and deeded to Alvarez Fisk around 1840. Tradition tells us that the home was "built to endure and determined not to fall," which has held true through the years. At one time it was the Stanton College for Women.

The massive stone pillars and double galleries present a magnificent front entrance. Long referred to as the old Fisk home, it has been restored by the American Legion. Private.

Wall Street at High Street in Natchez.

Clifton Site

Mention must be made of the mansion that once stood on the site of Clifton Heights, a subdivision just north of downtown Natchez.

CLIFTON was built about 1815 by Samuel Postlethwaite, son-in-law of William Dunbar. Later it was acquired by Frank Surget, whose wife was Charlotte Linton, a celebrated hostess and wealthy in her own right. One can just imagine the elaborate parties given at the mansion.

CLIFTON and all of the outbuildings were completely leveled during the Civil War due to an oversight by Mr. Surget, who failed to invite a Union officer to a dinner party. The officer was so outraged by the slight that he ordered the home to be demolished. The story goes that not one brick was left standing in place.

The family was able to save some of the priceless treasures, but their losses weighed so heavily on their hearts that they soon departed to live in France. Unfortunately, Frank Surget died before leaving the country, but his wife lived on in Bordeaux, France, until her death many years later.

A section of Natchez today perpetuates the name of this beautiful home unnecessarily destroyed due to one man's animosity.

Clifton Heights in Natchez.

Commercial Bank

The facade of this stately building is gray-white marble with four Ionic columns. Other elevations are stuccoed brick.

Built in 1833 for the purpose of housing the COMMERCIAL BANK, it is now, after a sequence of other uses, the First Church of Christ Scientist.

For security reasons a banker's residence was usually constructed in connection with the bank. This home may be viewed around the corner on Canal Street.

206 Main Street in Natchez. 🏛

Concord Site

Although CONCORD is among the "lost mansions" of Natchez, mention must be made of this historically important home. In the late 1700s, when the Natchez country belonged to Spain, Don

Gayoso de Lemos, a charming diplomatic gentleman, welcomed Americans into the territory, and CONCORD became the center of a lavishly entertained provincial society.

Gayoso built the home in the 1790s. It was an enormous structure of Spanish design, with three levels and galleries on all sides. After it was destroyed by fire in 1901, all that remained were two graceful curving stairways which were removed in recent years for safety purposes.

The home was occupied by Winthrop Sargent when he was territorial governor and later purchased by Don Esteban Minor (Stephen Minor of Pennsylvania), who had served as an official under the Spanish rule.

The visitor should know about the historical significance of this site, and be reminded of the brilliance of Natchez society at the turn of the nineteenth century.

Off Pine Ridge Road in Natchez.

Cottage Gardens

The earlier type of provincial architecture, which was supplanted by the later colonial mansions, is noted in COTTAGE GARDENS, with its spaciousness and wide veranda with six large square columns. The beautiful doorway enters a large central hallway with an unusual stairway.

Built in the 1790s, it was at one time the residence of Don Jose Vidal, a young nobleman and last acting Spanish governor of Natchez, whose tomb may be seen in the Natchez cemetery. Private.

Myrtle Avenue between Oak and Elm streets in Natchez.

Coyle House

This attractive two-story residence with brick construction below and wood above is simple in appearance and classic in design. Built between 1793 and 1797, the house has been preserved by the Natchez Historical Society. Private.

300 block South Wall in Natchez.

D'Evereux

D'EVEREUX is said to be the official Natchez example of classic Greek architecture. Dating from 1840, it was designed for William St. John Elliott and was the scene of magnificent entertaining. With large rooms and wide galleries, the home occupies a perfect site on a hillside and was chosen, at one time, as the most perfect home, in style and setting, in the entire South.

Henry Clay was a frequent visitor in this lovely home, and thousands of twinkling candles burned at the gala balls given in his honor.

It is tastefully decorated and in an excellent state of preservation.

Overnight accommodations. Call (601) 446-6631; out-of-state, (800) 647-6742; ask for bed-and-breakfast department.

U.S. 61 (North), in Natchez. 🏠

Dixie

Perfectly restored in 1963-64 is the one-story red brick cottage, DIXIE. The home was originally built in two sections, the oldest dating back to 1795. The front section, with a portico supported by four columns and surrounded by wood railings, was added when the property was acquired by Samuel Davis, older brother of Jefferson Davis. Private.

211 South Wall in Natchez.

Dr. Dubs' Townhouse

Dr. Charles Dubs, a native of Philadelphia who moved from New Orleans to Natchez, built this two-story brick house in 1852. The typical nineteenth-century townhouse has a recessed Greek Revival doorway with narrow sidelights and transom.

DR. DUBS' TOWNHOUSE is furnished with antiques from famed craftsmen, with emphasis on rare Southern period pieces. Private.

311 North Pearl Street in Natchez. 🏠

Dunleith

Dunleith

One of the most palatial and picturesque mansions in Natchez is DUNLEITH, built in about 1856 for Charles Dahlgren and his wife, Mary Routh Dahlgren.

Routhland, an earlier home on this 700-acre Spanish land grant, was destroyed by fire when it was struck by lightning in 1845. The stables and other outbuildings date back to the Spanish era of the late 1700s.

The present structure, approached by a circular drive, is completely surrounded by galleries supported by twenty-six colossal cement-covered brick columns. The upper balconies are decorated with lacy iron grillwork.

The interior was planned in keeping with the grand manner of the golden age of Natchez. Large rooms, with floor-length windows and beautiful furnishings, provided luxury and comfort to the owners and their guests.

Several generations of the Carpenter family occupied DUNLEITH, a magnificent home that will remind the visitor of a Greek temple.

Open to the public Monday-Saturday, 9-5; Sunday, 12:30-5; nominal entrance fee. Call (601) 446-8500. Overnight accommodations. For reservations call (601) 446-6631; out-of-state, (800) 647-6742; ask for bed-and-breakfast department.

Homochitto Street near Arlington Avenue in Natchez.

Edgewood

The unique feature of this large, stuccoed home is that, architecturally, it does not resemble any of the other houses built in Natchez in the mid-nineteenth century. Constructed in the early 1850s by Samuel Lambdin and his wife, née Jane Bisland, on a portion of the original 1786 Bisland estate, the home reflects the simple taste of the builders.

Edgewood

The two-storied front features a single-story porch with eight Corinthian columns. Overlooking a slope, the back of EDGE-WOOD has three levels, the lower one originally housing the kitchen. The furnishings include many valuable pieces of rosewood and mahogany, which enhance the charm and beauty of the house, both inside and out. Private.

Airport Road (off Pine Ridge Road) north of Natchez.

Elgin Plantation

This comfortable, rambling, old-fashioned home dates back to antebellum days when it was owned by the Dunbar family and named ELGIN (with a hard *g*) for the ancestral estate in Scotland.

"Sir" William Dunbar never claimed the title of his father, and the story is told that when he ordered a new coach from the East, he specifically requested that a monogram, not a coat of arms, be placed on the door of the carriage.

His country estate, "The Forest," is one of the "lost mansions" of Natchez, having been destroyed by fire before the Civil War.

Many generations of the Dunbar family have lived at ELGIN, a lovely home surrounded by a forest of oaks and pecan trees.

Overnight accommodations. For reservations call (601) 446-6631; out-of-state, (800) 647-6742; ask for bed-and-breakfast department.

Elgin Road off U.S. 61 (South), near Natchez.

The Elms

This wide, rambling two-and-a-half-story home is one of the oldest and most representative of the Spanish era of Natchez, dating back to the late 1700s. Its galleries, encircling three sides of the house, have iron grillwork banisters. The most distinguishing feature of the pink stucco building is the elaborate wrought-iron stairway which was once outside and is now incorporated into the central hall.

The Elms

For many years, it was known as the old Drake home, owned by the descendants of Benjamin Drake. Drake was the president of Elizabeth College, which held the distinction of being the first college in the nation to permit the teaching of higher education to women. Private.

215 South Pine in Natchez. 🏛

Elms Court

ELMS COURT, in a natural wooded setting, is one of the loveliest antebellum homes in Natchez. It was originally built in 1810 for Louis Evans, first sheriff of Adams County.

Multimillionaire Frank Surget bought the home in the early 1850s for his daughter, Jane, and her husband, Ayres P. Merrill, who later was appointed U.S. minister to Belgium by President U.

S. Grant. The Merrills changed the architecture from Spanish colonial to Italianate, with exquisite lacy iron grillwork along the double galleries. Still later, James Surget acquired the property for his daughter Carlotta and her husband, David McKittrick.

ELMS COURT contains priceless heirlooms from many generations of the Surget family. Private.

John R. Junkin Drive off U.S. 61 (South), in Natchez. 🏠

Elward

In the mid-nineteenth century, many cottages were built along quaint Washington Street. A fine example is ELWARD, a charming one-and-a-half-story red brick home surrounded by a trim lawn and white picket fence. Private.

612 Washington in Natchez.

Evans-Bontura

EVANS-BONTURA is a two-and-a-half-story brick home with the upper and lower front galleries lavished with railings of very unusual ornamented ironwork, resembling a New Orleans Creole townhouse.

Parts of the present house were built in stages between 1851 and 1858 by Robert D. Smith, a free man of color. Records show that the property was acquired in the mid-nineteenth century by Don Jose Bontura, a tavernkeeper.

The home commands a splendid view, situated on Broadway where fabled Silver Street rises from "Natchez-under-the-hill," the latter having been mostly claimed by the ever-changing course of the Mississippi River. In time, all that will remain of the lower town will be the recorded history and many legendary tales told about the riotous living on the waterfront.

The house is owned by the National Society of Colonial Dames of America in the State of Mississippi.

107 South Broadway in Natchez. 🏠

Fair Oaks

Dating from 1822, FAIR OAKS is a fine example of the Southern planter's home. It is a one-and-a-half-story white frame, roomy house with a ninety-eight-foot veranda supported by hand-hewn cypress columns. The wooden-peg construction testifies to the age of this beautifully preserved home. Private.

U.S. 61 (South), near Natchez. 🏠

First Presbyterian Church

The FIRST PRESBYTERIAN CHURCH of Natchez was formally organized in 1817. The original sanctuary was built on a high hill in 1815. In 1828-29 the hill was graded to its present level and a much larger church was built which forms, essentially, the present sanctuary. Other additions were made in 1830 and 1851 to this beautiful structure.

400 State Street in Natchez.

The Gardens

With a sloping roof extending over the veranda, THE GARDENS is an excellent example of early Spanish architecture.

Jefferson Davis is reported to have been a guest in this home the night before his marriage to Varina Howell at the Briars.

For many years the house was the residence of Louise-Clarke Pyrnelle, noted author of *Diddie, Dumps and Tot,* a Southern classic reprinted by Pelican Publishing Company in 1973. Private.

Out Cemetery Road in Natchez.

Glenburnie

An important example of Mississippi home building before the dominance of the Greek Revival style, GLENBURNIE was constructed in about 1833, and was extensively altered and added onto between 1901 and 1904.

Nestled in a wooded park, the house is built on Spanish lands granted to Adam Bingaman in 1798. Private.

John R. Junkin Drive in Natchez. 🏛

Glenfield

GLENFIELD, a one-story brick home of Gothic design, was built by Charles Green in 1812 on part of an original Spanish land grant. The house, situated in a shaded area among vine-covered hills and bayous, was named Glenncannon by an earlier owner, William Cannon.

The peaceful setting was interrupted by flying bullets during the Civil War, and the battle scars remain. Serenity has returned to this old place in spite of the traffic noises from a nearby busy intersection. Private.

Government Fleet Road in Natchez.

Glenwood Site

Mention must be made of GLENWOOD, one of the lost antebellum homes of Natchez. It was the home of Richard Dana, an eccentric aristocrat and talented musician, and his guardian, Miss Martha Dockery.

When a murder occurred in the neighborhood, the two recluses were accused but found not guilty. GLENWOOD'S trespassing goats—allowed to roam the area—had caused dissension between the parties involved. The goats were housed inside GLENWOOD, giving it the nickname "Goat Castle."

Left undisturbed for so many years, the old home finally gave way to a new subdivision, a sad ending to a once proud home.

Near the intersection of U.S. 61 (South) and U.S. 61 (By-pass) in Natchez.

Gloucester

Gloucester

Most authorities agree that this handsome, three-level, solid red brick home was built for David Williams in 1800. A member of the Williams family, Maria McIntosh Williams, who later became the wife of Winthrop Sargent, the first governor of the Mississippi Territory, occupied the home.

In 1808, Governor Sargent made several changes in the original plan of this home and developed the surrounding plantation acreage and gardens. A unique feature is its octagonal shape. The house includes a basement with heavy barred windows and doors, surrounded by a dry moat. Typical of this period are the front and back galleries.

Upon the death of Governor Sargent in 1818, his only surviving son inherited the home. He was later murdered by Union soldiers when he opened the front door to offer them the hospitality of GLOUCESTER. His bloodstains remain today.

Fine marble mantels, crystal chandeliers, priceless paintings, mirrors, and a collection of first-edition books are a few of the elaborate furnishings which have remained in this elegant home through the generations. Private.

Lower Woodville Road in Natchez.

Grand Village of the Natchez Indians

While driving around modern Natchez, approximately three miles from the downtown area, the visitor should be aware of the historically significant site on St. Catherine's Creek. This was the Grand Village of the Natchez Indians, first described by d'Iberville in 1700.

Fort Rosalie was established here after the First Natchez War in 1714. Historians Le Page Du Pratz and Dumont de Montigny described the attack and massacre of the fort in 1729 and the eventual abandonment of the village in 1730.

In the flatbottom land on the west side of the creek are three burial mounds, one almost eliminated by stream erosion. The village, covering approximately five acres, was situated on the east side of the creek. Today a museum displays excavated artifacts, renovated Indian mounds, a reconstructed hut, and other interpretive exhibits illustrating the village's life-style. Wooded nature trails traverse the area.

Open Monday-Saturday, 9-5; Sunday, 1:30-5. Admission free. Call (601) 446-6502.

Off U.S. 61 South at 400 Jefferson Davis Boulevard in Natchez.

Green Leaves

GREEN LEAVES, built before the War of 1812, is a large cottage representing the comfort and beauty that early Natchezans incorporated into their homes, signifying luxury without ostentation. Shaded by century-old live oaks and magnolias, the home contains rare museum pieces of mahogany and rosewood furniture in palatial-sized halls and rooms.

GREEN LEAVES has been occupied by the Koontz and Beltzhoover families for many generations. Private.

303 South Rankin in Natchez. 🏛

The William Harris House

THE WILLIAM HARRIS HOUSE was built in 1834-35 by William H. Harris, an early merchant who, with his brother Ezekial Harris, had a store in "Natchez-under-the-hill." William Harris was also the father of General Nathaniel Harrison Harris of the Confederate Army.

The house is one of only two antebellum homes remaining in Natchez originally built with a brick ground story and a wooden upper story. It is furnished with period English and American antiques. Private.

311 Jefferson Street in Natchez. 🏛

Hawthorne

The history of HAWTHORNE is sketchy, but it is believed that this quaint Southern planter-type cottage, located on the old trace, now situated near a major Natchez intersection, was built around 1814. At one time it belonged to the Overaker family and later to the Dunbar family.

After many years of complete disrepair, it has been restored, with every historical detail preserved. The one-and-a-half-story, dormered, white frame house, with the typical broad veranda, stands proudly once again. Private.

Lower Woodville Road in Natchez. 🏛

Holly Hedges

Built in the 1790s by Don Juan Scott, HOLLY HEDGES was remodeled in 1830 following the popular Greek Revival architectural influence. Judge Edward Turner, early Natchez jurist, presented the house to his daughter and son-in-law, the John T. McMurrans, who later built their mansion, Melrose.

It is beautifully restored and furnished with priceless antiques. The interesting front steps lead to an attractive entrance and fanlight doorway. Private.

214 Washington Street in Natchez.

Governor Holmes House

This two-story red brick house dates from 1794 and has retained the name of one of its earlier owners, David Holmes, the last governor of the Mississippi Territory and the first governor of the state of Mississippi.

It has been beautifully restored in keeping with the simplicity of its early provincial architecture. Private.

200 block of South Wall in Natchez.

Hope Farm

This picturesque home is one of the oldest in the city. Records show that the original portion, the English wing, was built around 1775. The front, of Spanish colonial architecture, with a broad, comfortable veranda, was added by Governor Don Carlos de Grande Pre, probably around 1790. Seven solid cypress columns support the low sweeping roof.

For many years the Montgomery family owned the house, which was later purchased and restored to its present beauty by the Balfour Millers. The spacious rooms are filled with rich mahogany, applewood, and rosewood furniture, heirloom silver, family portraits, and lovely crystal and china.

In the spring the gardens are indescribably beautiful with massive azaleas, dogwood trees, and tulips in full bloom.

Hope Farm

Former resident Mrs. Katherine Grafton Miller is credited with originating the famous Natchez Pilgrimage in the 1930s, and her home is truly exemplary of the history, the graciousness, and the beauty which abound in the city. HOPE FARM is now the home of Mrs. Ethel Green Banta and family.

Overnight accommodations. Call (601) 446-6631; out-of-state, (800) 647-6742; ask for bed-and-breakfast department.

147 Homochitto Street at Duncan Avenue in Natchez.

The House on Ellicott's Hill

The sturdy, quaint old structure standing high atop Ellicott's Hill was known for many years as Connelly's Tavern. Owned by the

The House on Ellicott's Hill

Natchez Garden Club, it is one of the most important landmarks in the state of Mississippi.

It was here that Andrew Ellicott, tavernkeeper, raised the first United States flag, in February 1797, over the District of Natchez. The exact date of construction is unknown, but most historians agree that this perfectly proportioned building was probably erected around 1795. The style of architecture is early Spanish, made of brick and timbers said to have been salvaged from abandoned sailing vessels.

There are many stories to tell about the famous guests of the tavern. Among them were Aaron Burr and Blennerhasset, who met here in secret to discuss Burr's ill-conceived plan to carve an empire out of the Southwest United States.

The building stands proud and well preserved today and is a "must" on the itinerary of the Natchez visitor.

Open to the public daily, 9-4:30. Nominal entrance fee. Call (601) 442-2011.

200 North Canal in Natchez.

50

King's Tavern

King's Tavern

Known also as the Bledsoe house, the earliest records show that ownership of this structure was transferred to Richard King in 1789 and it is considered by many to be the oldest building in the state of Mississippi.

King became a tavernkeeper in the days when the weary traveler needed a well-fortified haven against Indian outbreaks. Built of brick, ship timber, and cypress, its resemblance to a blockhouse of pre-Revolutionary days gives credibility to its age.

Among the notable historical events that have occurred at the tavern are the frequent meetings which Aaron Burr held with his associates. The first United States mail, brought over the Natchez Trace by an Indian runner, was delivered to and distributed from this old place.

Descendants of Samuel Postlethwaite, early Natchez settler, lived under its roof for six generations. It is now owned by the Pilgrimage Garden Club. Private.

613 Jefferson in Natchez. 🏛

Lansdowne

This spacious, comfortable Georgian home, dating from 1853, has a large portico enclosed by intricate grille railings. The graceful front steps lead down to the old carriage blocks.

The interior displays the original Zuber wallpaper, rosewood and mahogany furniture, portraits of the members of the Marshall family, lovely china, silver, and other family heirlooms.

Charlotte Hunt Marshall, the first mistress of LANSDOWNE, was the daughter of David Hunt, who made possible the Chamberlain-Hunt Military Academy in Port Gibson. David Hunt was at one time one of the wealthiest men and largest slaveholders in the nation. Private.

Out Pine Ridge Road, near Natchez. 🏠

Leisure House

Known also as the Griffith-McComas house, this charming residence is of the modified West Indies design with upper and lower porches that run the width of the house. It was built during the Spanish era of Natchez in 1794-95.

The attractive entrance is enhanced by a lovely fanlight doorway. A bookshop was once operated on the lower floor by Mrs. Harold Leisure.

Open to the public.

301 South Wall in Natchez.

Linden

The exact origin of LINDEN is lost in history, but there are records dating back to 1790. It was once the home of the Thomas Feltus family, descendants of William Conner, who owned and occupied the home for several generations.

The center section is two-storied with single-story apartment wings on each side. A broad gallery, ninety-eight feet in length, enhanced by beautiful white columns, spans the entire front.

Linden

The rooms are spacious, elegant, and comfortable. The doorway, with its delicate fanlight, is probably the most beautiful in Natchez.

LINDEN houses many rare and exquisite furnishings and art treasures, among them three original paintings by Audubon and a portrait of Jenny Lind.

The driveway that encircles the home, well-kept gardens, and giant moss-laden oak trees provide a setting for this old house which the visitor will long remember.

Overnight accommodations. Call (601) 446-6631; out-of-state, (800) 647-6742; ask for bed-and-breakfast department.

Linden Drive, off Melrose Avenue, in Natchez. 🏛

Longwood

The story of LONGWOOD is a sad one. It is an unfulfilled dream of a man, Dr. Haller Nutt, whose wish was to live and entertain in a stately mansion of Moorish design. After years of plan-

Longwood

ning, importing European mantels, stairways and statues, and investing more than one hundred thousand dollars, the construction was abruptly halted when the Civil War began.

The home, now owned by the Pilgrimage Garden Club of Natchez, stands among giant oaks and moss-tangled woods, just as it was when the workmen put down their tools so many years ago and answered the call to arms.

LONGWOOD is castlelike, the largest octagonal house in the United States, with six levels, including the dome at the top. Plantation-burned bricks, handcarved grillwork, and time-enduring cypress timber were used in the construction.

Dr. Nutt was a wealthy planter and scientist of international renown. He went abroad to study the cotton crops of Egypt and while there became fascinated with the Moslem palaces. Upon his return he retained Samuel Sloan, a noted Philadelphia architect, to plan this magnificent home.

When the war began, the family moved into the basement, the only completed section of the house. Dr. Nutt, an ardent Unionist, died in 1864. His courageous wife and eleven children remained at LONGWOOD and carried on in the tradition of the Southern aristocracy.

This imposing structure has long been referred to as Nutt's Folly, but the visitor has only to drive through the wilderness setting and encounter this breathtaking mansion which stands like a vision from the pages of *The Arabian Nights* to understand his love for the place.

Open to the public daily, 9-5; nominal entrance fee. Call (601) 442-5193.

Lower Woodville Road in Natchez. 🏛

Magnolia Hall

MAGNOLIA HALL, one of the finest examples of the Greek Revival style in Natchez, was built in 1858 by Thomas Henderson, a wealthy planter, merchant, and cotton broker. The well-proportioned portico is dominated by four massive Ionic columns.

The house has been restored by the Natchez Garden Club. The downstairs rooms of the mansion are filled with antiques much like those that would have been present in the mid-nineteenth century. The second floor houses Natchez' only costume collection.

Open to the public daily, 9-4:30; nominal entrance fee. Call (601) 442-6672.

215 South Pearl Street in Natchez. 🏛

Melmont

MELMONT is a sturdy, two-story structure with decorative double front galleries, built before the Civil War by Henry B. Shaw for his bride, Mary Elizabeth Lattimore.

Much thought went into the naming of an estate, and MELMONT was no exception. The young mistress chose the initials of her maiden name, *MEL,* and added *MONT* for the rolling elevation on which the home stood. Private.

715 North Rankin in Natchez.

Melrose

The visitor approaches MELROSE along a circular drive which passes a tranquil pond lined with old cypress trees. In this beautiful setting, the imposing two-story brick Georgian mansion exemplifies the glamor of antebellum Natchez. Huge double parlors and an adjoining library allowed ample space for elaborate entertaining.

Built in the early 1840s for Judge John T. McMurran, law partner of General John A. Quitman, the home is in a perfect state of preservation with several outbuildings still in use.

Beautiful rosewood furniture, gold-leaf mirrors, brocade draperies, lovely chandeliers, priceless china, and silver pieces are among the treasures the visitor may see in this home. The old punkah is suspended over the dining table.

In 1866 Judge McMurran lost his life when the steamboat *Fashion* was destroyed by fire at Baton Rouge. George Malin Davis had acquired the property the previous year, and his descendants resided at MELROSE for many generations.

Open to the public daily, 9-5; nominal entrance fee. Call (601) 442-8224. Overnight accommodations. For reservations call (601) 446-6631; out-of-state, (800) 647-6742; ask for bed-and-breakfast department.

Melrose Avenue near Ratcliff Place. 🏠

Mississippi Bank

This unpretentious building once housed the first territorial bank in Natchez. It was given a monopoly as the official state bank in 1818, after Mississippi became the twentieth state in the Union in 1817.

The Planter's Bank purchased the site in 1831.

334 Main Street in Natchez.

Mistletoe

MISTLETOE is one of the well-preserved Natchez homes which belonged to the prominent Bisland family. It was built in the early 1800s by John Bisland for his son and daughter-in-law, Peter and Barbara.

Designed along simple lines, this sturdy frame house was constructed with hand-hewn timber and wooden pegs. The entrance is across a wide front porch with four square columns and wooden railings. The doorway features a lovely transom and sidelights, and the home is filled with antique treasures. Private.

Airport Road off Pine Ridge Road, north of Natchez.

Monmouth

This imposing Greek Revival two-story brick mansion has large square pillars supporting the double portico. The doors, fanlights, sidelights, and window frames are all of handcarved wood.

The home, like its former owner, General John A. Quitman, is solid, substantial, and somewhat awesome. It stands as a monument to one of Mississippi's best-loved citizens. Eliza and John Quitman acquired the property and surrounding acreage around 1826.

General Quitman won military distinction during the Mexican War. He later became a member of the U.S. Congress and governor of the state of Mississippi. In 1859, he and other guests were mysteriously poisoned at a dinner given for President Buchanan in Washington, D.C. Quitman died many weeks later at his beloved MONMOUTH.

Open to the public daily, 9:30-4:30; nominal entrance fee. Call (601) 442-5852. Overnight accommodations. For reservations call (601) 446-6631; out-of-state, (800) 647-6742; ask for bed-and-breakfast department.

Main Street near Melrose Avenue in Natchez.

Montaigne

Montaigne

A reminder that Natchez had more millionaires than other cities in the nation at one time is manifest in MONTAIGNE. It is a home of classic beauty surrounded by enormous azaleas and other flowering shrubs that are the photographer's delight in the spring.

It was built in 1855 for Confederate General William T. Martin, whose features are carved on Stone Mountain in Georgia, representing the state of Mississippi. MONTAIGNE takes its name from the French Huguenot word for Martin.

It is said that horses were stalled in the parlors, the rosewood furniture used for kindling, and the silver melted by Union soldiers while they occupied MONTAIGNE during the Civil War.

Handsomely restored, it stands today a solid two-story structure built of the sturdiest timber, undaunted by the ravages of time and the desecrations of war. Private.

200 Liberty Road in Natchez. 🏠

Mount Repose

Mount Repose

William Bisland, country gentleman, cotton planter, and prominent citizen of Natchez, built this large frame home in the 1820s.

The main portion is two-storied with double galleries and several wings, making the home comfortable and spacious. An interesting story is told that William Bisland believed so strongly that Henry Clay would become president of the United States that he lined the front drive of the property with oak trees and openly declared that it would remain closed until Clay became president. To this day the house is approached from the side, the front gate remaining unopened through all the years.

A well-known member of the family was the author Elizabeth Bisland, a close associate of Lafcadio Hearn. Descendants of the Bislands still reside at MOUNT REPOSE.

Overnight accommodations. Call (601) 446-6631; out-of-state, (800) 647-6742; ask for bed-and-breakfast department.

Out Pine Ridge Road, north of Natchez.

Myrtle Terrace

MYRTLE TERRACE, built in the 1830s, is a small, compact cottage with a big history that belongs, in part, to Captain Thomas Leathers. Captain Leathers was a man of big stature and big ideas, the most noted of which was the famous *Natchez-Robert E. Lee* steamboat race from New Orleans to St. Louis in 1870.

Legend tells us that Captain Leathers, of the *Natchez*, lost the race not because he had a slower boat, but because, in his overconfidence, he nonchalantly made all of the scheduled stops and then refused to jeopardize the safety of his passengers by overpressing the boilers. This colorful hero in the history of Natchez lived at MYRTLE TERRACE for many years.

The home, attractively restored, is situated high on terraced ground surrounded by azaleas and other foliage which are in full bloom in the spring. Private.

310 High Street in Natchez.

Oakland

OAKLAND was built in the mid-1830s for Catherine Chotard Eustis, granddaughter of Major Stephen Minor (Don Esteban), last governor of the Natchez District under Spanish rule. Descendants of the Minor family resided here for generations.

Standing in secluded woods, the house was built for comfort. With simplicity of design, OAKLAND resembles the typical Southern planter's house and is representative of the restoration in which local residents participate to keep their heritage alive.

The one-story sturdy brick home features a wide veranda with banisters and six columns. The interior holds many family treasures and antiques. Private.

Oakhurst Drive off Old Pond Road in Natchez. 🏛

Natchez Cemetery

Overlooking the Mississippi River, on hills and terraces landscaped with stately live oaks, magnolias, crepe myrtle, sweet olive, and many other Southern plantings, is the Natchez cemetery. The site, which included approximately ten acres of the estate of John Steele, was chosen in 1822.

Many of the earlier graves have caved into a deep bayou to the south. Some of the oldest tombs are found in the rear, many of these dating from the 1820s. These were removed from the center of Natchez where St. Mary's Cathedral is now located.

Early prominent Natchez citizens buried in the cemetery are Lyman Harding, counsel for Aaron Burr at the latter's trial under the oaks in nearby Washington in 1807; Judge Edward Turner; General John A. Quitman; Colonel Henry Chotard, who served with Andrew Jackson at the Battle of New Orleans; General W. T. Martin, hero of the Confederacy; and colorful Captain Tom Leathers, of the steamboat *Natchez*.

Still another marker simply states, "Louise the Unfortunate," believed to be a young girl who had died of tuberculosis in a house of prostitution in "Natchez-under-the-hill."

The grave of a Beekman child, the only casualty of the Civil War within the limits of the city, may be seen. She was killed by a shell fired from a Union gunboat.

On the south side is a tall shaft of Carrara marble inscribed "Don Jose Vidal, born in Spain in 1765." His remains were moved here by his son-in-law, Samuel Davis.

Cemetery Road in Natchez.

The Parsonage

This sturdy brick home has a story that is unique. Peter Little, master of Rosalie, built THE PARSONAGE in 1840 for one purpose—to have privacy in his own home. Eliza, his young zealous wife, was so enthusiastic about religion that she invited every itinerate preacher and his family to share the hospitality of her home. After a particularly long period of constant houseguests, Mr. Little built a house across the street to accommodate her friends in the ministry. In 1850 he deeded it to the Methodist Church and called it THE PARSONAGE.

The Parsonage

After the death of his young wife, Peter Little, a lonely broken old man, was murdered in the seclusion of his home by one of his own slaves.

Today the house, with exquisite antique furnishings, is the residence of the Orrick Metcalfe family, descendants of early Natchez settlers. Private.

305 South Broadway in Natchez. 🏛

Pleasant Hill

PLEASANT HILL was built in 1803 and is still occupied by descendants of the Postlethwaite family, the original owners. By today's standards this spacious home would not be considered a cottage, but it was in the days of enormous mansions with eighteen-foot ceilings.

In the mid-nineteenth century the house was moved from a high elevation one block north to its present location, and the "pleasant hill" was leveled.

Overnight accommodations. Call (601) 442-7674.

310 South Pearl in Natchez.

Presbyterian Manse

Sitting high on a terraced elevation is the PRESBYTERIAN MANSE, dating from 1820. It is a beautifully proportioned one-story dusty pink cottage featuring an exquisite doorway with transom. The women of the church have restored the interesting little study in the side yard with attention to every architectural detail. Private.

307 South Rankin in Natchez.

Priest House and Lawyer's Lodge

Dating back to the Spanish era, the two-story white frame PRIEST HOUSE and its one-story wing known as LAWYER'S LODGE are fine examples of the historic restoration that has been carried on by the Natchez Garden Club. They are situated adjacent to the House on Ellicott's Hill, and a parking area for visitors is in the rear of the buildings.

200 North Canal in Natchez.

Ravenna

This is the earliest documented Greek Revival residence in Natchez, with pillared double galleries both front and back, standing tall and dignified. Built in the 1830s by the Harris family, the home was unroofed during the disastrous tornado of 1840 which damaged nearly every home in Natchez and left several hundred citizens killed or injured.

The Metcalfe family acquired RAVENNA before the Civil War, and during the Federal occupation were ordered to vacate when Mrs. Metcalfe was suspected of communicating with the Confederate forces by way of the deep ravine that runs by the property.

The Metcalfe family maintained possession of the home for many years, and each generation must have felt a love of flowers, for masses of azaleas, wisteria, dogwood, and other flowering shrubs and plants present a spectacular panorama in the spring. Private.

South end of Union Street in Natchez. 🏠

Ravennaside

Built in the late nineteenth century by Mr. and Mrs. James S. Fleming, imposing RAVENNASIDE is surrounded on three sides by sweeping galleries. Mrs. Roane Fleming Byrnes, daughter of the builders, lived here and served as president of the Natchez Trace Association from 1935 until her death in 1970. Mrs. Byrnes played an important role in the mapping of the original Natchez Trace.

The house has been restored and contains many original furnishings.

Open to the public September through mid-June, daily, 9-5. Overnight accommodations. Call (601) 442-8015.

601 South Union Street in Natchez. 🏠

Richmond

RICHMOND has probably been studied by architects and historians more than any other house in Natchez. It was built in three distinct sections representing three eras of Natchez history, with Spanish, Greek Revival, and Georgian architectural influence.

The original section, now the middle of the home, was constructed around 1770 with hand-hewn timber, brick, and cement. Sturdily built, it has stood the ravages of time with no remodeling necessary.

Richmond

The Greek Revival wing, which is now the front entrance, was built in 1832 by Levin R. Marshall, a wealthy planter and banker, whose descendants still occupy the house.

At the rear of the home, the Georgian wing was erected in 1860. Constructed with hand-burned plantation red brick, the rooms were planned with high ceilings, large windows, and spaciousness to accommodate the growing Marshall family and numerous houseguests. The roof of the front gallery is supported by classic Corinthian columns. Inside, the broad hallway opens to large double parlors and dining rooms.

One of the oldest and largest homes in the area, RICHMOND holds many priceless treasures. Among them are a carved rosewood piano used to accompany the famous Swedish singer, Jenny Lind; an ornate coin-silver service; the original massive furniture; old laces; candelabra; and an 1850s model bathtub. The visitor can glimpse a wide scope of Natchez history while enjoying the beauty of this gracious old home. Private.

Government Fleet Road off John R. Junkin Drive in Natchez.

Rosalie

Situated high on a bluff, 200 feet above the Mississippi River, is ROSALIE, a two-story red brick antebellum mansion. The front portico is supported by four massive columns. The choicest home-pressed bricks and hand-hewn timbers were used in its construction, which began in 1820 and required seven years to complete.

ROSALIE bears the name and is near the site of Fort Rosalie, built by the French in the early 1700s. It is believed that the home is also near the area of the great Indian massacre of the French in 1729.

History abounds in the halls of this old home. The original owner, Peter B. Little, married his thirteen-year-old ward, Eliza Low, and sent her to Baltimore to complete her education. He built ROSALIE for her during this period.

During the Civil War, the Andrew L. Wilsons owned the home. Mrs. Wilson, a Southern sympathizer, was eventually exiled to Atlanta for the duration of the war. President Jefferson Davis dined at a lovely mahogany table that is still displayed. Later the home was the headquarters of Ulysses S. Grant during the Federal occupation of Natchez.

The present owners, the Mississippi Society, Daughters of the American Revolution, have preserved many of the original furnishings, among them the enormous four-poster, canopied bed in which General Grant slept during his residence at ROSALIE.

Open to the public Monday-Saturday, 9-4:30; Sunday, 1-4:30. Nominal entrance fee. Call (601) 445-4555.

100 Orleans in Natchez.

Routhland

ROUTHLAND is a beautiful Southern plantation home situated on a high elevation overlooking acres of natural woods. It was built in 1817 on land that belonged to the original Routh (pronounced Ruth) holdings. The home features a spacious veranda, ten slender columns, an attractive doorway with sidelights and transom, and graceful front steps.

The home has been beautifully restored and modernized but contains many lovely antiques befitting its place among prominent Natchez antebellum homes. Private.

92 Winchester Road in Natchez. 🏠

St. Mary's Cathedral

The history of this imposing Gothic cathedral began with the laying of the cornerstone in 1842 by Bishop John Chanche. The bishop, during his earlier priesthood in Maryland, had administered last rites of the Church to the one surviving signer of the Declaration of Independence, Charles Carroll. He labored endlessly for the completion of the new church, and on Christmas Day 1843, the rough, crude building with primitive furnishings was blessed.

In 1858, under Bishop William Elder, the present floor was laid, beautiful carved woodwork installed, and the present arched ceiling constructed.

During the Civil War the bishop refused to take orders in the matter of public prayer and was exiled to a military prison in Vidalia, Louisiana. Seventeen days later the cathedral bells rang when he was returned to his post in Natchez.

More beautiful and elaborate additions have been made through the years, and today St. Mary's stands as an important landmark in the history of Catholicism in Mississippi. Visitors welcome.

107 South Union in Natchez.

Saragossa

The age of this simple yet elegant old home is unknown. Its Spanish architecture, almost primitive in design, attests to its age.

The wide verandas around the house indicate the foresight the builder had to assure the occupants the maximum of shade and cooling breezes in the days prior to modern air-conditioning.

The home is situated in a secluded natural setting beneath moss-draped live oaks and Southern plantings. Private.

Lower Woodville Road in Natchez.

Shields Town House

This home, the last fine town house built in Natchez before the Civil War, was completed in 1860. In 1869 William Shields purchased the residence, which remained in the Shields family until 1912.

The house is a graceful example of late Greek Revival residential architecture.

Overnight accommodations. Call (601) 446-6631; out-of-state, (800) 647-6742; ask for bed-and-breakfast department.

701 North Union Street in Natchez. 🏛

Stanton Hall

In the heart of Natchez stands the most palatial residence in the city, STANTON HALL, built in 1858. This imposing antebellum home is probably the most expensive home built during the golden era of cotton. The iron fence, with its delicate design, in itself is worth a fortune. The builder, wealthy Frederick Stanton from Belfast, Ireland, chartered an entire ship to bring materials and furnishings from Europe for his showplace.

The facade of the three-level home features four enormous Corinthian columns supporting the double galleries encircled with lacy ironwork.

The interior, with vast halls and eighteen-foot ceilings, has double drawing rooms and a music room which can be opened to form a seventy-two-foot ballroom. The stairway, an example of architectural genius, rises three flights in a series of elliptical curves. Its balustrades and mahogany rails are handcarved. In the Carrara marble mantels, bronze chandeliers, and other elaborate appointments, STANTON HALL attained the ultimate in lavish, yet tasteful decor.

This mansion, which well represents the grandeur of the Old South, may be seen through the continuing efforts of the Pilgrimage Garden Club.

Open daily, 9-5; nominal entrance fee. Overnight accommodations. For reservations call (601) 446-6631; out-of-state, (800) 647-6742; ask for bed-and-breakfast department.

401 High Street in Natchez. 🏠

Stanton Hall

Texada

Built in 1792, this two-and-a-half-story red brick structure is one of the largest townhouses built in the early years of Natchez. Occupied by Don Manuel Texada from 1797 to 1817, this large home, with no architectural adornment, is still known as TEXADA.

Overnight accommodations. Call (601) 446-6631; out-of-state, (800) 647-6742; ask for bed-and-breakfast department.

222 South Wall in Natchez. 🏠

The Towers

In 1840 the lovely acreage on which THE TOWERS now stands was deeded to G. O. Blenis by Dinah Postlethwaite, early Natchez family member. Other owners included George Dicks and William C. Chamberlain, who in 1859-60 remodeled the house in the design of an Italian villa. The front entrance, unlike any other in Natchez, has recessed double galleries—the lower level featuring three beautifully detailed arches, the upper level, intricate ironwork railings. The twin towers at the third level were destroyed by fire a number of years ago.

At this time the road to town was nothing more than a bridle path through woods over to Clifton and North Pearl Street. The home was known at that time as Gardenia, for the cape jessamine along the walks in the garden. A summerhouse stood in a sunken area, and a pool was surrounded by hedges of Cherokee roses, shaded by giant oaks and cypresses. Acacia and hibiscus enhanced the beauty of this noted garden.

Mr. Chamberlain, who never lived in THE TOWERS, the house of his dreams, sold it in 1861 to John Fleming, just before war broke out. A descendant of John Fleming, after other changes in ownership, restored the home to its original beauty.

Probably the most interesting historical incident occurred when Captain Peter B. Haynes, a sensitive Union officer quartered here, was not invited to an elegant dinner given by the Surgets and in a rage gave the order to destroy their palatial mansion, Clifton.

Many of the furnishings from the Fleming ancestral home in Alexandria, Virginia, may be seen in the Natchez homes of the Fleming descendants. Private.

801 Myrtle Avenue between Oak and Elm in Natchez.

Trinity Episcopal Church

This beautiful church houses the second oldest Episcopal congregation in the state of Mississippi, and its sanctuary is the oldest church building in Natchez. In 1821, as a result of a meeting in the home of Dr. Stephen Duncan at Auburn, the church was formally organized. The building was begun in 1822; the first services held in 1823.

It has been remodeled only twice through the years—in 1839 when the dome was removed and the roof line reduced to its present level, and in 1883 when the recess chancel was added with the beautiful LaFarge window.

305 South Commerce in Natchez.

Twin Oaks

A Natchez home that has been restored to its original beauty is TWIN OAKS, standing on an original land grant to Jeremiah Routh, a prominent early settler.

Shaded by ancient live oaks, the exterior of the one-and-a-half-story white cottage features the typically inviting front porch with banisters and four large columns.

The house dates from between 1810 and 1814 and has had numerous owners and occupants. Mother Cornelia Connelly, founder of the Society of the Holy Child Jesus, lived here from 1832 until 1835. Federal troops occupied it during the Civil War.

During the restoration the hardware on the doors was discovered to be of solid silver.

Twin Oaks

Overnight accommodations. Call (601) 446-6631; out-of-state, (800) 647-6742; ask for bed-and-breakfast department.

71 Homochitto at Arlington Avenue in Natchez. 🏛

Van Court Townhouse

This home, featuring an attractive entrance with wrought-iron grillwork, is a two-and-a-half-story brick and frame home with the typical architecture of the townhouses of that period. Servants quarters are to the right of the main house. Private.

Washington Street at Union Street in Natchez.

Villa Lombardo

This old two-story brick home, one block from the river, was once situated at the hub of activity along the river and the trace.

Beautiful exterior features are the intricate iron balcony and exquisite gate. The shuttered building is otherwise without adornment.

It now houses a large collection of antiques and many Natchez items. Private.

300 North Canal in Natchez.

Weymouth Hall

Dating from 1850, WEYMOUTH HALL, a large two-story home with double galleries both front and back, was the home of Colonel John Weymouth.

Located high on a bluff overlooking the Mississippi River, this grand old home features a captain's walk which, with its strategic location, made it most suitable for Federal occupancy during the Civil War. Stark Young mentions WEYMOUTH HALL several times in his famous novel about Natchez, *So Red the Rose.*

The most interesting feature of the interior is a black marble mantel inlaid with mother-of-pearl.

Open to the public daily, 9-5; entrance fee. Overnight accommodations. Call (601) 445-2304.

Cemetery Road in Natchez.

The Wigwam

The oldest portion of this interesting and unique house dates back to the late eighteenth century and is definitely considered to be one of the oldest homes in Natchez. The wings were added later. It is reported to have been built originally on an Indian burial mound and appropriately named THE WIGWAM.

The exterior features an attractive recessed entrance with delicate iron grillwork. The home is approached by a circular drive through the lovely landscaped lawn. Private.

Oak Street between Maple and Myrtle avenues.

Williamsburg

Built shortly after 1830, this one-and-a-half-story frame home is an excellent example of the Federal-style cottage in the Natchez area, with especially fine architectural details. Of particular interest is the dado paneling on the front gallery and the dormers with semicircular transoms.

WILLIAMSBURG was built by John Baynton, a prominent Natchez attorney who married into the wealthy Sessions family. Private.

821 Main Street in Natchez. 🏛

Jefferson College

Formerly Jefferson Military Academy, JEFFERSON COLLEGE is one of the most historically significant sites in the state. Founded in 1802, it is one of the oldest boys' schools in the United States. It was here that the constitution for the new state of Mississippi was

Jefferson College

74

written in 1817. One of its most distinguished students was ten-year-old Jefferson Davis. John James Audubon was on the faculty at one time.

Near the front gate are two giant live oaks, known as the Burr Oaks, under which the trial of Aaron Burr, arraigned for treason, was held.

Continuing restoration of the site is under the auspices of the Mississippi Department of Archives and History.

Nature trails and picnic facilities are available. Several historic buildings are open to the public; a visitor center is located in Prospere Hall. Buildings open Monday-Saturday, 9-5; Sunday, 1-5; grounds open dawn to dusk. Admission free. Call (601) 442-2901.

In Washington, six miles east of Natchez. 🏠

Propinquity

The architecture of this large, unadorned two-story frame home, dating from 1810, is the simple early American style, built for spaciousness and comfort.

Brigadier General Leonard Covington, commander of a troop of Light Dragoons at nearby Fort Dearborn, appropriately named his home PROPINQUITY because his property was adjacent to the fort. In the early days the naming of homes and plantations was a great event, and in many cases names have been carried on by tradition despite many changes of ownership.

Later, for many generations, PROPINQUITY was owned and occupied by descendants of Jane Long, known as the "Mother of Texas" because of her support of her husband's expedition to Texas in the early nineteenth century. Private.

Near Washington.

Natchez Trace

THE NATCHEZ TRACE was once an Indian path, then a wilderness road between Natchez and Nashville, and from 1800 to

Natchez Trace

1830, a highway binding the old Southwest to the Union. The TRACE has been a vital factor in the growth of the nation. Today markers, exhibits, and trail markers explain why this frontier road has been remembered and preserved.

Brandon Hall

This large antebellum home was built in 1856 by the third generation of Brandons. The first, Gerard Brandon, an Irishman, came to Natchez before the American Revolution and acquired the property known as Selma Plantation, which had one of the original pecan groves in the country.

It is a large house, with many galleries and tall chimneys. The timbers are secured with wooden pegs. Private.

Off the Natchez Trace Parkway, north of Washington.

Emerald Mound

Covering nearly eight acres, EMERALD MOUND is the second largest Indian temple mound in the United States. Built and used between A.D. 1300 and 1600 by forerunners of the Natchez tribe, the mound measures 770 by 435 feet, with a 35-foot-high first level and a 30-foot secondary level. A climb to the peak offers a beautiful view of the area.

At the lower end of the Natchez Trace Parkway, north of Washington.

Mount Locust

The smell of sweet olive and burning wood out back at MOUNT LOCUST takes the visitor into history—the history of the Natchez Trace. This inn, one of the oldest along the famous path, dates from 1777 and was one of the first stops on the trail that men followed back east after coming down the river by boat with their merchandise. An exhibit shelter, adjacent to the parking area, traces the history of the structure.

At the lower end of the Natchez Trace Parkway, north of Washington.

Springfield

SPRINGFIELD, one of the largest and most elaborate residences of its time, is a two-story Southern planter's home, built in 1791 by Thomas Marston Green, Jr., territorial justice of the peace. It is said to be the site of the wedding of Andrew Jackson and Rachel Robards.

Open to the public daily year-round, 10-6 in spring and summer; 10:30-5:30 in winter. Overnight accommodations and group tours available. Entrance fee. Call (601) 786-3802.

Ten miles west of Fayette on Mississippi 553 near Church Hill.

Oakland Chapel

Built in 1830, now beautifully restored OAKLAND CHAPEL is located on the campus of Alcorn State University. The school was established as Oakland College, the first state and federally supported black college in the United States.

The magnificent front steps that lead to the main floor of the imposing three-story structure are reported to have come from the Windsor mansion.

Six miles west of Lorman on Mississippi 552. 🏛

Old Country Store

The visitor must pause and browse in this original old general store, established in 1875 and continually operated since that time. One of the state's oldest businesses, it has been featured in many periodicals and newspapers.

The building was constructed in 1890, and its floors are worn uneven by five generations of customers. An authentically preserved structure, it has many of the original fixtures and memorabilia from the nineties.

Open Monday-Saturday, 8:30-6; Sunday and holidays, noon-5. Closed Easter and Christmas. Call (601) 437-3661.

U.S. 61, ten miles south of Port Gibson at Lorman.

Rodney

RODNEY was a bustling river town in the 1800s that became a ghost town when the river changed its course. A few old buildings and two interesting churches, the Rodney Presbyterian Church and the Sacred Heart Catholic Church, are all that stand as reminders of a thriving community in which Jefferson Davis, Zachary Taylor, and Andrew Jackson were frequent visitors.

The two churches are listed on the National Register of Historic Places.

West of Lorman on Mississippi 552, then left at Alcorn State University on a local paved road.

Laurel Hill

The approach to LAUREL HILL is through a deeply cut road shaded by massive old trees. The large white two-story frame structure, built between 1815 and 1820, has double galleries with balustrades and seven-and-a-half-foot-thick walls.

The most unusual feature of the interior is the closed staircase, which is unlike the beautiful stairways in large central halls of other homes of the period.

Dr. Rush Nutt, the builder of LAUREL HILL, was well known for his experiments in agricultural science and improvements in farm implements, as well as for his participation in the civic affairs of the territorial and early statehood days of Mississippi. His son, Dr. Haller Nutt, built Longwood in Natchez. Private.

Two miles southeast of Rodney. 🏛

Bethel Presbyterian Church

As an undisciplined column of Union soldiers marched toward Port Gibson on May 1, 1863, they took aim and peppered away at the steeple of this sturdy old Presbyterian church dating from the 1820s.

South of Windsor ruins on Mississippi 552.

Windsor

Twenty-two huge Corinthian columns are all that remain today of WINDSOR, a magnificent mansion. Completed in 1861 by Smith C. Daniell, a wealthy planter, the home had five levels topped by an observatory.

Windsor

Windsor Castle, a nickname given to it by the slaves, was later the home of another wealthy aristocrat, David Hunt—owner of twenty plantations and 1,700 slaves—believed to have been the largest slaveholder in the South.

The home was destroyed by a fire of unknown origin in 1890.

West of Port Gibson on Mississippi 552, four miles east of the river. 🏛

Port Gibson Area

Introduction

The land on which Port Gibson stands was once a part of the mighty Choctaw nation. The little Southwest Mississippi town that Ulysses S. Grant labeled "too beautiful to burn" has many lovely old homes and churches.

The first white community in the area that is now Claiborne County was near Pettit Gulf, just north of Rodney, a hunting settlement in the early eighteenth century. In 1802 the county was organized and named for W. C. Claiborne, governor of the territory. It was the third county formed in the state.

Samuel Gibson acquired a large tract of land from the Spanish government on the south fork of Bayou Pierre. By 1788 a permanent settlement had grown around the boat landing of his plantation, known as Gibson's Port or Gibson's Landing. In 1811 the name was officially changed to Port Gibson. Bayou Pierre was then navigable for flat boats and small boats at certain times of the year. Often when these boats were unloaded, they were dismantled and the materials used for home construction—some of which are still in existence.

The visitor will enjoy a motor tour of this historic town with its beautiful homes and landmarks. Port Gibson hosts an annual spring pilgrimage of homes. For information about homes open for tours, visitors should contact the Port Gibson-Claiborne County Chamber of Commerce, P.O. Box 491, Port Gibson, Mississippi 39150.

Disharoon House

This very large, comfortable two-story frame home with wide upper and lower galleries dates from the early 1830s. A beautiful interior feature is the spiral stairway extending up three floors.

81

Disharoon

Gibson's Landing, a bed-and-breakfast hotel, is operated in the house.

Open to the public by appointment; nominal entrance fee. Call (601) 437-3432.

1002 Church Street in Port Gibson.

Englesing

Englesing

Built in 1817, this quaint story-and-a-half frame cottage is one of the oldest structures in Port Gibson and was occupied by the Englesing family for several generations. Of special note in the side yard is the oldest formal garden in the state of Mississippi. Private.

702 Church Street in Port Gibson.

Gage Home

When the visitor catches sight of the GAGE HOME, a lovely old two-story frame house with wide, comfortable galleries situated in the heart of town, it is easy to see why General Grant labeled Port Gibson as the town "too beautiful to burn."

The two-story brick building on the left of the property served as the kitchen and servants quarters during antebellum days. The home, dating from the 1830s, has been kept beautifully restored.

Open to the public by appointment. Nominal entrance fee. Call (601) 437-5239.

602 Church Street in Port Gibson.

Gage Home

Idlewild

Idlewild

This charming antebellum raised cottage, in a picturesque land-scaped setting, was built in 1833. Of unusual interest are the twelve-foot doors and windows. Private.

U.S. 61 south of Port Gibson.

McGregor

McGregor

Built in 1830, this fine antebellum home features fourteen-foot ceilings and jib doors under the windows. Private.

Mississippi 547 in Port Gibson.

Methodist Church

Port Gibson's METHODIST CHURCH was organized in 1804. The present structure dates from 1860.

In Port Gibson.

Miss Phoebe's

This charming cottage, built in about 1811, is one of the oldest homes in Port Gibson. The property and furnishings in the house have been in the same family since the early 1800s. Private.

705 Farmer Street in Port Gibson.

Oak Square

The massive oak trees surrounding this Greek Revival home gave OAK SQUARE its name. Built in 1906, the house recreates the splendor of southern Mississippi antebellum architecture. Overnight accommodations. Call (601) 437-4350.

Church Street in Port Gibson.

Person Home

Built in the 1880s, this Queen Anne-style house features a lavish display of stained glass on the facade. Private.

Church and Chinquepin streets in Port Gibson.

Planters Hotel

Established in 1817, the old PLANTERS HOTEL must have accommodated many weary travelers when Port Gibson was an active trading center on the south fork of Bayou Pierre. The hotel was restored as a private home and is now an office building.

Main Street in Port Gibson.

Presbyterian Church

Presbyterian Church

One of the most photographed historic churches in the state, the PRESBYTERIAN CHURCH was organized in 1807; the present structure dates from 1859.

The most unique feature is the hand pointing toward heaven at the top of the steeple.

Church Street in Port Gibson.

St. James Episcopal Church

ST. JAMES was formally organized in 1826. The present structure dates from 1884.

In Port Gibson.

St. Joseph's Catholic Church

In the heart of Port Gibson is ST. JOSEPH'S CATHOLIC CHURCH, built in 1849. It features beautiful paintings by Thomas Healey and intricate Daniel Foley carvings.

Church Street in Port Gibson.

Spencer Home

Spencer Home

This home is a good example of the sturdy and lasting quality of construction in the early days of Mississippi. Built in 1830, the woodwork and flooring are of solid cypress. An unusual feature is the quaint stairway. Private.

1302 Church Street in Port Gibson.

Temple Gemiluth Chassed

The Mississippi Department of Archives and History maintains that this unusual structure, built in 1891, is the only one of its architectural style in the state.

Church Street in Port Gibson.

Van Dorn House

This old place was probably built about 1830. Due to its location, with a commanding view on the south side of town, it was commonly called the Hill.

The house is two-story, L-shaped, double brick, and a combination of Georgian and Southern colonial architecture.

It was built by Peter A. Vandorn (his spelling), born in 1773, who established himself as a prominent lawyer and merchant in Port Gibson before 1820. He was married to Sophie Donelson Caffery, a niece of Rachel Jackson, wife of Andrew Jackson.

Their son, Earl Van Dorn, was born in 1820 and spent his early childhood at this family residence. He later won acclaim as a hero in the Mexican War and the Civil War with a rank of major general. His raid at Holly Springs gave the Union army one of the most severe defeats that it received in the state of Mississippi. The house, in a state of disrepair for many years, is being restored. Private.

Van Dorn Drive in Port Gibson. 🏛

Wintergreen Cemetery

The oldest marked grave in this old cemetery is that of a child buried in 1802. It lies in the plot of Samuel Gibson, the founder of the city. Of interest is the grave of Confederate general Earl Van Dorn, who was buried facing south.

In Port Gibson.

Canemount Plantation

CANEMOUNT, built in about 1855, is considered to be one of the finest examples of the Italianate revival influence in Claiborne County.

Open to the public by appointment. Call (601) 877-3784.

Mississippi 552 West, approximately fifteen miles from Port Gibson.

Old Wheeless Home

This log cabin was built between 1820 and 1825 by Green Berry Wheeless, who came to Claiborne County from Georgia.

The cabin has been covered with siding and has a tin roof, but the original construction may be seen on the interior and underneath the house. Private.

West of Port Gibson on the Port Gibson-Alcorn Road.

Grand Gulf Military Park

Once the scene of Civil War battles, the GRAND GULF MILITARY PARK covers 104 acres and has a museum and visitor center. Interesting relics on the grounds include wagons, buggies, a

Confederate caisson, and gun emplacements. The site of Fort Wade is within the park, and the ruins of Fort Cobun are nearby.

Visitors will see an ancient cemetery for a once-thriving community, long deserted and mostly in ruins.

Open year-round, 8-5; admission free.

Northwest of Port Gibson. 🏛

Rocky Springs

Of special interest to historians is the ghost town of ROCKY SPRINGS, a thriving community in the nineteenth century. All that remains is a church, still in use. A nature trail leads to the historic townsite, and a section of the old trace may be explored, bringing back visions of the harshness and dangers of the pioneer days when travelers hoped to avoid encounters with such outlaws as Murrell, Hare, and the Harpes. The site is administered by the National Park Service.

Campgrounds and picnic area.

Twelve miles northeast of Port Gibson on the Natchez Trace Parkway.

Rosswood

ROSSWOOD was built in 1857 by David Shroder, architect of Windsor, for Dr. Walter W. Wade. This Greek Revival home is situated on a 100-acre tract and is constructed mainly of cypress, with heart of red pine flooring.

The house has been designated a Mississippi Landmark.

Open to the public daily, 9-5; nominal entrance fee. Overnight accommodations. Call (601) 437-4215.

Mississippi 552 East, near Lorman. 🏛

Vicksburg Area

Introduction

One of the most historically interesting cities in the nation is Vicksburg, the scene of a forty-seven-day siege during the Civil War. It was labeled the Gibraltar of the Confederacy.

Today numerous homes, churches, and landmarks remind the visitor of the history and heritage of this city. The most noted attraction is the well-maintained Vicksburg National Military Park and Cemetery.

For information about the annual spring pilgrimage, visitors should contact the Vicksburg Convention and Visitors Bureau, P.O. Box 110, Vicksburg, Mississippi 39181. Call (601) 636-9421; out-of-state, (800) 221-3536.

Anchuca

This stately two-story Southern colonial home was built before 1830 by J. W. Mauldin, one of the first selectmen for the new city of Vicksburg. The name *Anchuca* is an Indian word meaning happy home.

It is situated in the oldest part of Vicksburg on the original land purchased by the Reverend Newitt Vick for two dollars an acre.

Joseph Davis, elder brother of Jefferson Davis, was a later owner.

Open to the public daily, 9-5. Nominal entrance charge. Overnight accommodations. Call (601) 636-4931; out-of-state, (800) 262-4822.

1010 First East Street in Vicksburg.

Balfour House

Originally this two-story brick home faced south, but the front entrance was reversed when some of the property was sold and access to the structure changed.

The exterior design is a combination of Federal and Greek Revival influences with a Doric portico and gallery, one-fourth of which has been enclosed. An unusual architectural feature is the slanting roof on the south side and the horizontal roof on the north side of the house.

The house was built in 1835 by William Bobb. Ownership of the property dates back to Lucy Vick, a descendant of the Reverend Newitt Vick, founder of the city.

Tradition and legend are associated with BALFOUR HOUSE. During the Civil War, it was here that a gala ball was held on Christmas Eve 1862, at which time word was received by the Confederate forces that Union troops, under General Sherman, were advancing toward Vicksburg.

Emma Balfour's famous diary has been a primary source for much written history about the siege.

Open to the public daily, 9-5; nominal entrance fee. Call (601) 638-3690.

1002 Crawford Street in Vicksburg. 🏠

Cedar Grove

CEDAR GROVE, formerly known as the old Klein place, is one of the South's largest antebellum homes. It stands as a stately monument to the era of gracious living enjoyed during the early days of Vicksburg.

Four huge columns support the double galleries of this lovely mansion built by John A. Klein in the 1840s. The home is decorated with exquisite taste, featuring some of the original furniture, mirrors, silver, crystal, and china. There is a marble mantel in every room.

Jefferson Davis spent many hours at CEDAR GROVE, and several generations of prominent persons have danced in the elegant grand ballroom. General U. S. Grant slept in one of the enormous four-poster, canopied beds shortly after the surrender of Vicksburg in 1863. Scars remain from the devastation of the siege. A cannonball is embedded in the wall of the parlor, and a large hole was left in the floor when another cannonball crashed into the basement.

Open to the public daily, 9-5; nominal entrance fee. Overnight accommodations. Call (601) 636-1605; in Mississippi, (800) 448-2820; out-of-state, (800) 862-1300.

2200 Oak Street in Vicksburg.

Christ Episcopal Church

The oldest church in Vicksburg and one of the oldest structures is CHRIST EPISCOPAL CHURCH, originally a red brick building.

The cornerstone was laid in 1839, but a yellow fever epidemic and a fire delayed its completion until 1843.

1115 Main Street in Vicksburg.

The Corners

Built in 1872, the architecture of THE CORNERS is an interesting combination of Victorian and Greek Revival, a raised cottage sitting high on a terraced lawn with a brick retaining wall and an attractive wrought-iron fence and gate.

John A. Klein, early Vicksburg planter and businessman, gave the home to his daughter, Susan, as a wedding gift.

The interior of the home, which has been featured in *House and Garden,* contains many beautiful antique furnishings in a modernized setting.

Open to the public daily, 10-5; nominal entrance charge. Overnight accommodations. Call (601) 636-7421; out-of-state, (800) 444-7421.

601 Klein Street in Vicksburg. 🏛

Duff Green House

Lacy iron grillwork columns and railings adorn the front double galleries of DUFF GREEN HOUSE, a beautiful example of Greek Revival architecture.

Built in 1856, the home served as a Confederate hospital during the siege, while its mistress, Mrs. Green, took refuge in a nearby cave and gave birth to a child, appropriately named Siege Green. Open to the public daily, 9-5; nominal entrance fee. Overnight accommodations. Call (601) 636-6968; (601) 638-6662.

1114 First East Street in Vicksburg. 🏛

Firehouse Gallery

The quaint old firehouse, which dates from 1870, will bring back memories of bygone days. The building has a meeting hall above the old stables. The exercise yard has been converted into a charming landscaped patio. Owned by the City of Vicksburg, the firehouse is the site of semi-annual art exhibits hosted by the Art Association.

1204 Main Street in Vicksburg.

Floweree House

This splendid two-and-a-half-story brick home overlooks the floodplains of the Mississippi River. The facade features an enormous portico with paired brick columns, and attractive entrances at both levels consisting of paneled doors with sidelights and transoms.

Superb craftsmanship is evident in the interior, including spacious and well-proportioned rooms, an interesting stairway, and elaborate rococo plasterwork. It is believed that Bavarian immigrants, a large number of whom were living in the area at the time, are responsible for the detailed workmanship.

The home, dating from 1877, was originally the residence of Colonel Charles C. Floweree, who, at the age of twenty, was the youngest officer of that rank in the Confederate army.

94

At one time the property was allowed to fall into disrepair, but it has now been restored.

Overnight accommodations; no public tours. Call (601) 638-2704.

2309 Pearl Street in Vicksburg. 🏛

The Galleries

The visitor will at once recognize the architecture of THE GAL-LERIES as that of a Louisiana raised cottage with its broad double galleries and its look of comfort.

Dating from 1850, the interior features a thirty-eight-foot hall-way that rises to three levels, accented with an oval spiral stairway and double chandeliers.

The home is beautifully preserved and decorated. Private.

2421 Marshall in Vicksburg.

Grey Oaks

This unique home was originally built as a plantation home in Port Gibson in 1834. The house was dismantled and moved to its present site in 1940. Set among six acres of landscaped gardens, the facade of the home resembles "Tara," the fictional home of Scarlett O'Hara in *Gone with the Wind.*

Open to the public Monday-Saturday, 9:30-4:30; Sunday, 1:30-4:30; nominal entrance fee. Overnight accommodations. Call (601) 638-4424.

4142 Rifle Range Road in Vicksburg.

Holy Trinity Church

The first rector of HOLY TRINITY CHURCH was the Rever-end W. W. Lloyd, who served as a Confederate chaplain.

The church, built in 1870, features a roof of Belgian slate, beautiful stained-glass windows, and a free-turning cross on the top of the steeple.

Of special note is the window on the Monroe Street side that honors the memory of Confederate and Union soldiers who lost their lives in the Civil War.

900 South Street in Vicksburg.

William A. Lake House

This quaint antebellum cottage, now reduced to one level after a destructive fire in 1916, was once a large two-story home.

The house was originally owned by Judge William Lake, who was killed in a duel. His bereaved widow went into complete seclusion after the incident, and, according to legend, one can hear the rustling of her skirts and smell the fragrance of her perfume on quiet evenings. Private; open for special tours. Call (601) 636-5693.

Main at Adams streets in Vicksburg.

McNutt House

One of the oldest houses in Vicksburg was for ten years the residence of Alexander Gallatin McNutt, twelfth governor of Mississippi.

A simple two-story frame L-shaped dwelling, it was designed and altered with consideration for economy and utility; therefore it lacks the sophisticated flair that was the hallmark for so many antebellum townhouses. In the 1850s some Greek Revival moldings and mantels were added to the interior.

The history of the home began in 1822 when Washington Cook paid thirty-five dollars for the lot and built a small four-room house on it. McNutt purchased the property in 1829 and added the rear wing. The appearance has remained virtually unchanged since that time.

The Hamilton Wrights and their descendants were owners until 1965, when the Mississippi Historical Foundation of Vicksburg purchased McNUTT HOUSE. The first floor is now a private school. Private.

815 First East Street in Vicksburg. 🏠

McRaven

McRAVEN, secluded in a beautiful setting of magnolias, century-old live oaks, and flowering plants and shrubs, is unchanged since Civil War days. It was built in three distinct architectural periods. The first section dates from the late 1700s when the settlement was known as Walnut Hills. Stephen Howard acquired the home in 1836 and made additional changes as did John Bobb in 1849. The latter was killed by Union soldiers in the gardens of McRAVEN after the siege of Vicksburg.

McRaven

Many original furnishings remain in the home, including toys, a rosewood piano, and parlor set. Of special note in the interior design are the wall moldings, plaster medallions, the graceful stairway, and the chandelier in the dining room.

Open to the public fall and spring, daily, 9-5; Sunday, 10-5. Summer, daily, 9-6; Sunday, 10-6. Nominal entrance fee. Call (601) 636-1663.

1441 Harrison Street in Vicksburg. 🏛

Old Courthouse Museum

This majestic old building is situated on a high elevation overlooking the city of Vicksburg. Built by slave labor in 1858, it has withstood battles, weather, and time. Within the superstructure is one of the oldest functioning clocks in the nation. The museum

Old Courthouse Museum

houses one of the South's largest and most interesting Civil War collections, Indian displays, and a large research library.

Caves dug into the hillside near the building provided safety for the citizens of Vicksburg during the siege.

A National Registered Landmark.

Open to the public year-round, Monday-Saturday, 8:30-4:30; Sunday, 1:30-4:30; nominal entrance fee. Call (601) 636-0741.

1008 Cherry Street in Vicksburg.

Pemberton House

This imposing antebellum house, on a high terraced elevation, dates from 1836.

It served as the headquarters for Lieutenant General John C. Pemberton, commander of the Confederate forces during the siege of Vicksburg. Private.

1018 Crawford Street in Vicksburg. 🏛

Planters Hall

This sturdy red brick two-story structure was built in the early 1830s to house Vicksburg's first bank. Spacious living quarters upstairs were provided for the bank's president and his family.

Interesting interior features include a bank vault with thirty-inch brick walls reinforced with iron bars, and a trapdoor which conceals a narrow stairway to the basement wine cellar.

The bank was closed in 1838 and purchased by the McRae family.

It was shelled by Federal gunboats during the Civil War siege, but withstood major damage and later was used as headquarters for the Union army's General Dennis.

Restored in 1956 by the Vicksburg Council of Garden Clubs, it houses furnishings and exhibitions of early Americana and Civil War memorabilia.

Open to the public during Spring Pilgrimage; nominal entrance charge. Call (601) 636-9114.

822 Main Street in Vicksburg. 🏛

99

St. Francis Xavier Convent

Five Sisters of Mercy opened this convent in October 1860, and occupied the small building in the center of the block. In 1868 the present convent was completed in a Gothic Revival architectural design. Private.

1021 Crawford Street in Vicksburg.

Seargent S. Prentiss Building

The small building which was once the office of the glamorous lawyer and orator Seargent S. Prentiss dates from 1790, and its primitive design attests to its age.

Of brick and cypress construction, the ceilings are eight feet high on the ground level and twelve feet on the second floor. Private.

1010 Monroe Street in Vicksburg.

Tomil Manor

Thirty-two stained-glass panels make the interior of this early twentieth-century Spanish villa glow with colored light. Fine oak paneling and a spectacular staircase are notable interior details.

Open to the public daily, 9-5; nominal entrance fee. Overnight accommodations. Call (601) 638-8893.

2430 Drummond Street in Vicksburg. 🏠

The Martha Vick House

This small house was built in the 1830s for the unmarried daughter of Vicksburg's founder, Newitt Vick. It has been restored and furnished with eighteenth- and nineteenth-century antiques. A large collection of French paintings is displayed throughout the house.

Open to the public daily, 9-5; summer, 9-7; nominal entrance fee. Call (601) 638-7036.

1300 Grove Street in Vicksburg.

Illinois Memorial, Vicksburg National Military Park

Vicksburg National Military Park

The VICKSBURG NATIONAL MILITARY PARK is one of the nation's most carefully preserved battlefields—the site of the siege of Vicksburg which lasted from May 18 to July 4 in 1863. It contains 1,330 acres, including the National cemetery. The visitor center presents exhibits, information about the siege, and tour directions to the Union and Confederate lines, artillery batteries, forts, redoubts, redans, and trenches.

The park also encompasses 1,600 monuments and markers and twenty state memorials. Fort Hill affords a panoramic view of the old riverfront.

Open to the public year-round, 8-5; admission free.

Clay Street near I-20 in Vicksburg. 🏛

Immaculate Conception Catholic Church

This small building, formerly the Nativity of Blessed Virgin Mary Church, has served as a place of worship since it was established as a mission church of Vicksburg in 1871.

In Raymond.

101

Jackson House

This one-story home, with an attractive four-columned portico, is one of the oldest and most historic homes in the town.

In Raymond.

Magnolia Vale

This charming old home was built by James B. Fairchild before the Civil War. His descendants still occupy the attractive cottage that the Union troops left unharmed.

In Raymond.

Peyton House

John B. Peyton built this dormered one-and-a-half-story frame home with clapboard siding in the 1830s and named it Waverly. One of the early settlers of central Mississippi, he is considered the "Father of Raymond." Peyton was a member of the team that surveyed the land acquired from the Choctaw Indians in the Treaty of Doak's Stand in 1820, the treaty that resulted in the settlement of these farmlands.

In 1829 he cast the deciding vote that kept the capital of Mississippi from being moved to Clinton and as a result was challenged to a duel by Judge Isaac Caldwell. Caldwell was grazed by a bullet from Peyton's rifle.

The home has been substantially remodeled in keeping with modern times. Private.

Clinton Road in Raymond. 🏛

Raymond Courthouse

Built between 1857 and 1859 by slave labor, this magnificent edifice is listed in the National Archives as one of the most perfectly

Raymond Courthouse

constructed buildings in the United States. It serves jointly, with Jackson, as the county seat of Hinds County.

In Raymond.

St. Mark's Episcopal Church

This quaint church building was erected in 1854 by a membership that had been formally organized in 1837.

The church housed the *Hinds County Gazette* following the disastrous fire of 1858, in Raymond. It was used as a hospital for Union soldiers wounded in the Battle of Raymond, May 12, 1863.

In Raymond.

Mississippi College

MISSISSIPPI COLLEGE, founded in 1826, is the oldest institution of higher education in the state. The one pre-Civil War building still standing on the campus, Provine Chapel, is one of the most historic landmarks in central Mississippi. Numerous other buildings on the campus are more than a half-century old.

In Clinton.

Canton-Yazoo City Area

Introduction

Canton became the county seat of Madison County in 1840. Originally part of the Choctaw Indian nation, the area was situated north of Spanish West Florida and was claimed by Georgia until 1804 when ceded to the Mississippi Territory.

Pushmataha, a famous Choctaw chief, relinquished the Indian claim to most of this part of the state at Doak's Stand in 1820. The Third Choctaw Session of 1840 resulted in the present county boundaries.

Today Canton serves as the civic, cultural, recreational, and governmental center for Madison County with deep-rooted traditions and a proud heritage. The city sponsors a spring pilgrimage of homes. Contact the Canton Pilgrimage, P.O. Box 53, Canton, Mississippi 39046. Call (601) 859-3815 or 859-4719.

The Dinkins House

This late nineteenth-century Victorian house was built by Claude Cameron Dinkins for his bride, Sally Weathersby. The house, originally a small cottage, was enlarged to accommodate the six children born to their union. Private.

253 East Peace Street in Canton.

Grace Episcopal Church

This small Gothic structure was built shortly after the construction of the Chapel of the Cross at Mannsdale, which was completed in 1853.

The earliest service of GRACE EPISCOPAL CHURCH was held in 1840 by "Fighting" Bishop Leonidas Polk. The church was officially organized in 1848.

The noted English architect Frank Wills designed the historic edifice featuring many arches, pinnacles, and a tower.

161 East Peace Street in Canton.

Greaves Home

Completed shortly after the turn of the century and one of the most elegant mansions in Canton is the GREAVES HOME. This two-story structure of buff-colored brick and gabled Victorian roof has tall Corinthian columns rising two levels with smaller columns on the first-story veranda. The shutters and latticework are cypress.

A lovely winding stairway graces the front hall. Many beautiful interior appointments are carved in solid oak and walnut. The home contains large spacious rooms and eleven fireplaces. Private.

379 East Peace Street in Canton.

Heart's Content

A stately Greek Revival home built in the 1890s by Mrs. Elizabeth A. Priestly, HEART'S CONTENT was named by Mr. and Mrs. Louis Hossley, who purchased it in 1903. Corner fireplaces surrounded by mahogany and tile mantels are unusual features in this house. Private.

304 Peace Street in Canton.

Madison County Courthouse

The city of Canton, located near the Big Black and Pearl rivers and the Natchez Trace, was incorporated in 1836. The town square has been the hub of activity since that time. This magnificent county courthouse built in 1852 is a Greek Revival building with Doric columns. Constructed of brick, the low roof is crowned by a cupola and the grounds are enclosed by an old iron fence, enhancing its majestic beauty.

Town square in Canton.

Madison County Historical Museum

This was once the Madison County jail with the date 1870 clearly visible over the front entrance. The original cell block of the two-story brick structure is believed to date prior to 1870. It is situated adjacent to the oldest cemetery in the city and a restoration project is underway to preserve this historical landmark as a museum.

Open by appointment and on Flea Market Days in May and October. Call (601) 859-2460.

234 East Fulton Street in Canton. 🏠

Mosby Home

This magnificent two-story brick mansion was built in 1856 by Colonel William Lyons. The Mosby family, prominent residents of Canton for four generations, have occupied it since the yellow fever epidemic of 1878.

The exterior features intricate decorations of this Greek Revival structure. The four stately columns rise two levels with ornate railings on the balcony. The beautiful entrances at both levels are noteworthy.

The interior contains spacious rooms filled with antique heirlooms. Private.

261 East Center Street in Canton.

Parker Home

The PARKER HOME, built by Captain William Priestly in 1852, is one of three Priestly family homes in this area. The Priestlys were prominent early residents of Canton.

An interesting and unusual historical fact is associated with this house—it was probably used as a post office before the Civil War. In the third-story attic, sacks of mail have been found which include old letters and papers written prior to the war and never delivered.

The Parker family has owned and occupied the dwelling since 1915. Private.

155 South Liberty Street in Canton.

Shackleford Home

This two-and-a-half-story brick home was designed in the Federal style of architecture with simple yet classic lines. Built by Judge C. C. Shackleford in 1852, the clay for the brick was taken from Belhaven Hill and the owner's plantation lands.

A housewarming was held when the home was complete. For this gala occasion, barbecued sheep and steers stuffed with quail and other delicacies were served. The punch bowls were continually filled and a dance climaxed the celebration.

Rooms are twenty feet by twenty feet with high ceilings. The kitchen to the rear of the house was connected by a covered walk.

During the war it is said that General Sherman camped across the street under the old "Gwinner Oak."

In this gracious home most of the original furniture, china, and cut glass remain in the same elegant setting for which they were intended. There are century-old vases, hurricane shades, law books dated 1660, etched Bohemian glass decanters, and candlesticks. Private.

326 East Peace Street in Canton.

Tilda Bogue

Built by Nathan Pittman in the mid-1830s, this two-pen, story-and-a-half, log dogtrot house was moved from its original location and restored in 1981. Private.

On Davis Road, off Mississippi 51 in Canton. 🏛

Vanity Castle

This typically Victorian residence with much gingerbread trim was built in 1898 by Judge William H. Powell. The home is situated on an elevation far back from the street in a lovely setting.

VANITY CASTLE has been restored to its original beauty. Private.

450 East Peace Street in Canton.

Wohlden

WOHLDEN was built by Colonel D. M. Fulton during the 1820s and was owned by the Rucker family until 1968.

An interesting feature is the maze sidewalk leading to the entrance of the Italianate home with a flat-roofed observatory.

The interior plan is comfortable, spacious, and tastefully decorated. The original kitchen and other dependencies still remain on the property. Private.

239 East Center Street in Canton.

Chapel of the Cross

One of the most outstanding examples of nineteenth-century Gothic Revival architecture is the CHAPEL OF THE CROSS, property of the Episcopal Diocese of Mississippi. The small brick building measuring approximately twenty-three feet by seventy feet features a porch, nave, organ niche, chancel, and sacristy. The Gothic influence is manifest in the carved rosewood bishop's chair and altar rail, both imported from England. A baptismal font is carved from a single block of Italian stone.

The history of this small chapel began prior to the Civil War, when Mrs. Margaret L. Johnstone built it as a memorial to her husband, John T. Johnstone (1801-48). He had come from North Carolina in 1820 with his brothers Samuel and William, who were also prominent early settlers with extensive landholdings. John Johnstone built two magnificent plantation homes, Ingleside and Annandale, both destroyed by fire in the early 1900s.

The little rural church suffered from the economic consequences of the Civil War and for a period of time was deserted and in a state of disrepair. Through the efforts of the Dancing Rabbit Creek Chapter of the Children of the American Revolution and other organizations, it has been restored and designated as a national shrine. Today services are held on the second Sunday of each month and each year on Easter Sunday.

Mississippi 463 (six miles northwest of juncture with I-55). 🏛

Casey Jones Railroad Museum State Park

John Luther Jones, better known as Casey, was born in Southwestern Missouri on March 14, 1863. From his earliest years his ambition was to be a railroad engineer and in 1888 he became a fireman on the Illinois Central Railroad. His lifelong fulfillment was his promotion to engineer in 1890.

His name has become legend through the vivid description in song of *The Wreck of the Cannonball Express*. This museum honors Casey Jones and offers interpretive exhibits about railroading in Mississippi. A 1923 oil-burning steam engine is on display.

Open to the public Wednesday-Saturday, 9-5; nominal entrance fee. Picnic facilities. Call (601) 673-9864.

One mile north of Vaughan.

Rob Morris Little Red Schoolhouse

The small two-story red brick building in the Federal style dates from 1847. The structure was originally built to house the Richland Literary Society. An act of the state legislature later changed its name to Eureka Masonic College, although the school never became more than a high school. While serving as principal, Dr. Rob Morris conceived the idea for the organization of the Order of the Eastern Star, which he founded in 1850.

The ROB MORRIS LITTLE RED SCHOOLHOUSE was used as headquarters for Confederate forces during the Civil War and later was used as a public school. Now the property of the Grand Chapter of Mississippi, Order of the Eastern Star, the structure is being restored as an historical shrine.

Mississippi 17, about 4.5 miles north of the community of Richland in Holmes County. 🏠

Bowman House

This is one of several antebellum homes that has been preserved in Yazoo City, called the Gateway to the Delta.

The two rooms across the front and the porch blinds of this antebellum structure are part of the original home dating from 1852. The rear of the home has been remodeled. Private.

407 East Madison in Yazoo City.

Gilruth House

Built prior to the Civil War, this home was cut to pattern in Cincinnati, Ohio about 1847—then shipped downriver by steamboat and assembled on the site. The structure has served at various times as a home, hospital, and church. Private.

320 East Madison in Yazoo City.

The Hollies

The one-and-a-half-story cottage dating from the 1830s is an excellent example of pure Southern architecture constructed with cypress timber, wooden pegs, and square nails. Private.

521 East Broadway in Yazoo City.

Tyler House

The lower floor of this attractive home is of brick from the 1850s. The second level, constructed of cypress timber, was added in 1870. Private.

327 East Madison in Yazoo City.

Yazoo City Library

The YAZOO CITY LIBRARY is an outgrowth of the oldest library association in the state of Mississippi.

First named the Manchester Library Association, it was organized in September 1838. When the name of the town was changed in 1842 to Yazoo City, the library took the same name. Meetings of the association were initially held in the Armory Building and the old Presbyterian Church. Essays and debates by prominent citizens were on the program agenda. After using various other buildings, Mrs. B. S. Ricks presented the present building in memory of her husband in 1900. This structure houses more than 28,000 volumes.

310 North Main Street in Yazoo City.

Jackson Area

Introduction

In 1821 the legislature selected LeFleur's Bluff on the Pearl River as the state capital and changed the name to Jackson in honor of General Andrew Jackson. Today it is a metropolitan center for the ever-growing trade markets and expanding industries in the state.

During the Civil War, General William T. Sherman had the city almost completely burned and destroyed. The few remaining antebellum homes and buildings have been carefully preserved. Some are open to the public year-round, others during the spring pilgrimage.

Today this modern city, with its friendly citizens, offers a variety of interesting attractions.

City Hall

This magnificent structure, which commands a city block in downtown Jackson, dates from 1847. It was used as a hospital during the Civil War.

Open to the public Monday-Friday, 8-5; admission free. Call (601) 960-1530.

203 South President Street in Jackson. 🏛

Governor's Mansion

The GOVERNOR'S MANSION in Jackson is one of the most historic and majestic official residences in the United States. It was first occupied by Governor Tilghman M. Tucker in 1842 and since

113

Governor's Mansion

then has been the home of Mississippi first families, with the exception of the Civil War years, when it was the headquarters for General Sherman, and during Reconstruction.

A beautiful two-story brick building, painted white with a portico supported by four enormous Corinthian columns, it has been remodeled and beautifully decorated through the years. The original handcarved lintels and intricate handwrought moldings are still admired by visitors.

Prominent Americans who have been entertained at the mansion include Henry Clay, Theodore Roosevelt, President William Howard Taft, Eleanor Roosevelt, Queen Wilhelmina, and John F. Kennedy. The guestbook includes names from every state in the nation and many foreign countries.

Guided tours on the half-hour, Tuesday-Friday, 9-11:30. Admission free. Call (601) 359-3175.

Capitol Street in downtown Jackson. 🏛

Manship House

In a beautiful garden setting, the one-story frame MANSHIP HOUSE, dating from 1857, is of Gothic Revival architectural style, both the exterior and interior. The furnishings include a number of family heirloom pieces.

Manship House

Charles Manship, the builder, became one of Jackson's most distinguished business leaders. He served as mayor of Jackson in 1862-63 and surrendered the city to General Sherman on July 16, 1863.

Of particular note is the bell at the north side of the house. In 1881 the Jackson Volunteer Fire Department presented it to Manship, the sole survivor of that organization.

An adjoining visitor center displays Manship family memorabilia and nineteenth-century decorative arts. The house is operated by the Mississippi Department of Archives and History.

Open to the public Tuesday-Friday, 9-4; Saturday-Sunday, 1-4. Call (601) 961-4724.

420 East Fortification in Jackson. 🏠

Millsaps-Buie House

Built in the 1880s in Queen Anne style for Major Reuben Webster Millsaps, this two-story frame structure is situated on a high elevation facing west. The interior features ten-foot doors to the three formal rooms, with fourteen-foot ceilings, beautiful plaster medallions, and marble mantelpieces.

Reuben Millsaps distinguished himself in the business and financial world, as an honored civic leader, and as benefactor of Millsaps College in Jackson.

Overnight accommodations. Call (601) 352-0221.

628 North State Street in Jackson. 🏠

Mynelle Gardens

Beautiful azaleas, camellias, and other rare plants and trees surround two lovely houses in this park owned by the city of Jackson.

Built in 1917, the WESTBROOK FAMILY HOME is an Italian Mediterranean house. The interior is highlighted by imported mahogany paneling, while the patio, paved with Tennessee marble, is graced by a giant fig tree.

GREENBROOK, built in 1920, was the home of Mynelle Westbrook Green, the creator of the lush six-acre garden.

Open to the public daily, March 1-October 31, 9-6; November-February, 8-5. Closed January 1, Thanksgiving, and Christmas. Call (601) 960-1894.

4736 Clinton Boulevard in Jackson.

New Capitol Building

Mississippi's impressive statehouse, completed in 1903 at a cost of $1 million, is the product of a new century, a place of utility and

New Capitol Building

tradition. It is constructed of Bedford stone and is similar in design to the national Capitol. It stands with formal dignity on a commanding terrace in the center of downtown Jackson. The symmetrical building, four stories high, is surmounted by a high central dome and lantern and topped with a copper eagle that is covered with genuine gold leaf. The eagle stands eight feet high and has a wingspread of fifteen feet.

Tours by appointment Monday-Friday, 8-5; Saturday, 10-4; Sunday, 1-4. Closed January 1, Easter, Thanksgiving, and Christmas. Admission free. Call (601) 359-3114.

Mississippi Street between North President and North West streets in Jackson. 🏛

No Mistake Plantation

The house on this 2,000-acre plantation is the Smith family ancestral home. The acreage has been in continuous use, producing cotton, other crops, and registered beef cattle since 1835.

The exterior of the one-and-a-half-story cottage has a sloping dormered roof supported by eight columns on the broad veranda. Private.

On Mississippi 3 near Jackson.

The Oaks

Known also as the Boyd house, this cottage is a simple one-story clapboard dwelling with a recessed gallery across the east facade. Both the exterior and interior design follow the plain Greek Revival style of architecture. Only slight alterations have been made since it was built prior to the Civil War by James H. Boyd, a prominent Mississippi settler.

At the age of eighteen, Boyd migrated from Kentucky to Wilkinson County, where he and his brother published the state's first newspaper, *The Woodville Republican*. From there they moved to Bayou Sara, Louisiana, and operated a drugstore.

Records indicate that when he returned to central Mississippi, Boyd established the first drugstore in Jackson, in the mid-1830s, and distinguished himself as a businessman and civic leader.

In 1960 the structure was purchased and restored by the National Society of Colonial Dames of America, and it serves as state headquarters and a museum house.

Open to the public Tuesday-Friday, 10-4; Saturday-Sunday, 1-4; nominal entrance fee.

823 North Jefferson Street in Jackson. 🏛

The Oaks

Old Capitol Building

Old Capitol Building

The architecture of this Greek Revival structure encompasses the three orders of Greek architecture—Corinthian, Doric, and Ionic—the senate chamber, on the exterior side of the building, and the front portico respectively.

Begun in 1833, it was the seat of the state government from 1839 to 1903 and now serves as the State Historical Museum. Among prominent Americans who spoke here were Henry Clay, Andrew Jackson, and Jefferson Davis.

Open to the public year-round, Monday-Friday, 8-5; Saturday, 9:30-4:30; Sunday, 12:30-4:30. Admission free. Call (601) 354-6222.

Corner State and Capitol streets in Jackson. 🏠

Woodbine Place

A beautiful antebellum mansion, WOODBINE PLACE was built in 1840 by the Johnson family. The 1,280-acre plantation is owned and operated by the Jensen family in residence. Private.

Off Mississippi 433, out of Bentonia.

Sub Rosa

SUB ROSA is an unpretentious rural residence in the fertile farmland of northern Hinds County. It is a two-story frame structure of the provincial Greek Revival design adopted by many planters for spaciousness, comfort, and beauty.

The interior contains two elaborate mantels, interesting paneling, and solid cherry railings and newels in the stairway.

Although altered to accommodate modern living, the physical appearance of the home remains essentially the same as when it was built by John M. Greaves shortly after he arrived in Hinds County in 1836.

A large area of central Mississippi had been opened for development in the 1820s, and many settlers came—wealthy planters and small farmers alike—to better their fortunes.

Originally the property belonged to Thomas R. Burnham (1825). The Ellis S. Middleton family were later owners, and their descendants occupied the home until 1931.

The gracious country estate is considered a scenic showplace. Private.

Mississippi 49 in Pocahontas. 🏠

Hattiesburg Area

Introduction

Hattiesburg was founded in 1882 in the Choctaw Indian lands by Captain William H. Hardy, pioneer lumberman and civil engineer. The thriving city became a railroad center and in 1897 ushered in the lumber boom.

Many spacious cottages and magnificent mansions were built by the leaders of the community. Some of these ancestral homes are open to the public in the spring. The Hattiesburg Area Historical Society occasionally sponsors seasonal "Heritage Tours" of local homes, landmarks, and historical sites. The society will also provide guides to the area for tour groups. Contact the Hattiesburg Area Historical Society at (601) 583-1362, or the Hattiesburg Chamber of Commerce, P.O. Box 710, Hattiesburg, Mississippi 39403.

Bethea Home

This large, two-and-a-half-story home is surrounded by a lovely garden under towering trees. Its exterior features decorative front- and side-columned double porticos. Private.

131 West Eighth in Hattiesburg.

Cotten Home

This one-and-a-half-story home extends a gracious welcome to the visitor with its tree-shaded, terraced lawn and broad veranda that features wood railings and double pillars. Private.

210 Sixth Avenue in Hattiesburg.

Dunn Deane Borsage Home

This large two-and-a-half-story home features numerous manifestations of Gothic architecture in the many-arched gables, cupola, and bay windows. Private.

100 block of Short Bay in Hattiesburg.

Lyndhurst

Built in 1897, the charming one-story Komp-Bailey home features a many-gabled, dormered roof. An ornate veranda surrounds the entire front of the house. Private.

122 Short Bay in Hattiesburg.

Martin-Graves Home

This is a magnificent two-story mansion with a stately double-galleried portico and an attractive dormer window arrangement at the third level. Private.

600 Bay Street in Hattiesburg.

McLeod-Gilliam Home

The roomy, two-and-a-half-story McLEOD-GILLIAM HOME has many windows, cupolas, verandas, and all of the interesting decoration that epitomized the Victorian architecture of the 1890s.

The two massive camellia bushes on the front lawn were brought from Mobile by Mrs. John A. McLeod in 1897 and are believed to be the first of their species in Hattiesburg. The house is now an office building. Private.

802 North Main in Hattiesburg.

Pinehurst

In 1895 William H. Hardy, the founder of Hattiesburg, selected a beautiful spot on the western outskirts of town to build his home, which he named PINEHURST.

Thirty-three years later, W. D. Tatum built the present mansion at the same location. The home, in a lovely natural setting, is surrounded by pine and pecan trees. Marble steps lead to the portico, supported by stately columns.

Two generations of the Tatum family have acquired the antiques which furnish PINEHURST. Private.

110 Pinehurst Street, off Hardy Street in Hattiesburg.

Rush-Vickers Home

Comfortable and spacious, the RUSH-VICKERS HOME has typical wide galleries and a gabled roof with many dormers. The house is surrounded by aged shade trees. Private.

128 West Eighth Street in Hattiesburg.

Trinity Episcopal Church

Dr. William S. Simpson-Atmore, considered an authority on ecclesiastical architecture, organized TRINITY EPISCOPAL CHURCH in 1901 and modeled the structure after a Knights Templar Church in London, England. TRINITY was completed in 1912.

The nave is early English in style; the chancel is of Norman architecture; the twenty-nine lancet windows are of Munich antique cathedral glass. Many other windows, gifts from prominent people, add to the beauty of the building. All 400,000 bricks were laid by one member as his gift.

West Pine and First Avenue in Hattiesburg.

Turner Home

Built in 1904, the large, two-and-a-half-story TURNER HOME has an attractive Greek Revival exterior with its graceful Ionic front portico. Private.

500 Bay Street in Hattiesburg.

United States District Courthouse

The UNITED STATES DISTRICT COURTHOUSE in Hattiesburg is a one-story structure with a full basement and a granite foundation that supports a superstructure of marble walls and a tile roof. The facade of the former main entrance, on the northeast side, has eight Doric columns and double-hung windows with hinged transoms. The building, featuring many intricate and beautiful architectural details, was completed in 1910.

Its original purpose was to house the post office of the rapidly growing "hub city." Since 1933, it has accommodated the offices of various federal agencies and the district court.

South corner of Pine and Forrest streets in Hattiesburg.

Providence Baptist Church

PROVIDENCE BAPTIST CHURCH, which has played an important role in the lives of worshipers for generations, was organized in 1818 by eight charter members who had come to the area from Georgia and met to worship in an old log house.

In 1826 they built a church out of logs, and parts of that building stood until 1910. Providence is the second-oldest Baptist church in Mississippi. The present sanctuary was constructed in 1907.

Eatonville Road, approximately eight miles north of Hattiesburg.

Bounds Mill

Bounds Mill

Located near Heidelberg is the old gristmill built on Bounds Lake in the 1800s and still in operation.

In Vossburg, north of Laurel.

John Ford House

One of the most interesting old homes in the state—off the beaten path—is the JOHN FORD HOUSE. It is the oldest frontier-type home in the Pearl River Valley, built in the early 1800s by the Reverend John Ford, a Methodist minister who came to this area with his four brothers.

The first story of this three-level home is built of bricks which were made on the premises. The other two stories are constructed of heart pine, apparently handcut and hand-dressed. The sturdy old house, filled with primitive furnishings and utensils, gives visitors a true picture of the spirit of early Mississippians. Another version of the origin of the structure, possibly factual although not documented, is that it was built by a Spanish squatter in 1792 who sold it to Ford in about 1808.

In 1813 a stockade was built to protect the family and visiting travelers from marauding Indians, and the property became known as Ford's Fort.

Several important historical events took place here. Andrew Jackson and his staff, on their way to the Battle of New Orleans, were guests at the fort. Legend tells us that the Reverend Ford extended his hospitality only after Jackson agreed to use no profanity; the general's reputation for the use of salty language had preceded him.

The Pearl River Convention of 1816 met here when the north-south boundary line between Mississippi and Alabama was decided upon.

John Ford died in 1826 and his descendants retained ownership until 1962, when the home and six acres were acquired by the Marion County Historical Society.

Open to the public Saturday-Sunday, 1-5; nominal entrance fee. Also open by appointment; call (601) 736-8429.

On Mississippi 35, south of Sandy Hook (one-half mile south of the weighing station). 🏛

John Ford House

Gulf Coast Area

Introduction

Several interesting cities dot the Mississippi Gulf Coast between Bay St. Louis and Pascagoula. Situated among the pines, oaks, magnolias, Spanish bayonets, palmettos, and azaleas, the coast is the "Motherland of the Mississippi Valley," rich in the heritage and traditions of the Old South. Some of the cities are modern, thriving centers of business and industry, while others still step with the leisurely pace that the semitropical climate dictates. It is a place for relaxation and reflection.

Three-quarters of a century before the American Revolution, King Louis XIV of France sent the two explorer brothers, d'Iberville and Bienville, with a band of men in search of these shores, and here they established the first white settlement in 1699 at present-day Ocean Springs.

Many landmarks and comfortable homes of the past still remain despite the ravages of time and the occasional fury of a hurricane.

Many private homes are open to the public during annual spring pilgrimages, usually held in March or April. The Mississippi Gulf Coast Council of Garden Clubs hosts tours of area homes, gardens, and historical buildings. Specific information about Gulf Coast area pilgrimages may be obtained from the Mississippi Gulf Coast Convention and Visitors Bureau, Box 6128, Gulfport, Mississippi 39506-6128. Call (601) 896-6699; out-of-state, (800) 237-9493.

Breath Home

One of the oldest homes in Bay St. Louis is the BREATH HOME, built in the early 1800s. Julius Monet acquired the house in 1836. During the Civil War the family silver and other treasures were hidden from Union soldiers in the hollow of the huge oak tree that still stands today in the front of the home. Private.

616 North Beach (south of U.S. 90) in Bay St. Louis.

Cedar Rest Cemetery

This historic old cemetery, with raised tombs, is presently operated by the City of Bay St. Louis. The oldest marked grave is unknown, but it is believed that some graves date prior to the Civil War.

West side of Second Street, between Easterbrook and Main streets in Bay St. Louis.

Elmwood Manor

This stately old home was built in the early 1800s by Jesse Cowan. Construction was discontinued for several years during the War of 1812.

Shaded by century-old oaks, this large two-story brick house with double front galleries has a magnificent view of the bay. Private.

Corner of North Beach and Boardman (north of U.S. 90) in Bay St. Louis.

Our Lady of Gulf Church

The cornerstone of the original church at this site was laid in 1848. The church was destroyed by fire in the early 1900s. Construction on the present building began in 1908—an imposing structure designed in the Italian Renaissance style. Stained-glass windows were imported from Germany.

South Beach (near St. Stanislaus) in Bay St. Louis.

St. Stanislaus College

ST. STANISLAUS COLLEGE was founded in 1854 by the Brothers of the Sacred Heart, who had arrived in Mobile in 1846.

In 1870 the school was chartered as St. Stanislaus Commercial College and in 1923 became college preparatory, in which capacity it still exists.

There is an interesting blending of the old and the new in the buildings on this beautiful campus which overlooks the Gulf of Mexico. The older red brick buildings are Romanesque in design; the campus is shaded by ancient live oaks.

South Beach in Bay St. Louis.

Shrine of Our Lady of the Woods

In the center of what was once a dense forest is this very old shrine. It was built by Father Buteaux, an early church leader who had survived a shipwreck coming from France. This structure was erected in 1847 to show his thanks for salvation from drowning.

At the rear and east of Our Lady of the Gulf Church, South Beach in Bay St. Louis.

Ballymere

Surrounded by huge oaks and magnolias, BALLYMERE dates from 1839. It is the oldest house in Pass Christian and was originally used as a lighthouse.

With comfort in mind, the builder, unwilling to relinquish one breeze from the Gulf of Mexico, built his home 130 feet long and two rooms deep, extending the roof over the entire length of the veranda. All timber in the home is hand-hewn cypress. Private.

551 East Beach in Pass Christian.

Dixie White House

President Woodrow Wilson and his family were summer residents in 1913 at Pass Christian. Only a historical marker locates the site of the home, a large two-story raised cottage with a frame upper floor and brick basement, predating the Civil War.

767 East Beach in Pass Christian.

Frierson Home

The FRIERSON HOME is in a beautifully landscaped setting. The west cottage was built in 1835. The main house, which dates from 1885, features circular stairs. Private.

1024 West Beach in Pass Christian.

Gildersleeve Home

This charming two-story summer cottage was built by John Henderson between 1870 and 1875. At the turn of the century it was headquarters for the Louisville and Nashville Railroad. Private.

1001 East Beach in Pass Christian.

Live Oak Cemetery

Across the street from Trinity Church, in the same moss-draped surroundings, is the old cemetery, established in 1849. In it are the graves of many prominent settlers, including a great-granddaughter of Martha Washington and a grandniece of George Washington.

Church and St. Louis (near U.S. 90) in Pass Christian.

McCutchon Home

This home was built in 1849, a one-story cottage designed with Greek Revival influence. It was acquired by Samuel McCutchon in 1853. Frances Parke Lewis Butler, the descendant of Martha Washington, died in 1875 in the home and is buried in the Butler plot at Live Oak Cemetery. Private.

861 East Beach in Pass Christian.

Town Library

Although records only date back to 1893, the TOWN LIBRARY is known to have been in continual use for a much longer period; it is believed to be the oldest library on the Gulf Coast.

Open to the public.

221 Scenic Drive in Pass Christian.

Trinity Episcopal Church

One of the oldest church buildings still standing on the coast is TRINITY EPISCOPAL at Pass Christian. It is a small semi-Gothic structure which dates from 1849.

Constructed of cypress and pine timber, the sturdy little church has withstood the elements many times.

Interesting architectural features include beautiful memorial windows and quaint shuttered ventilators.

Church and St. Louis (near U.S. 90) in Pass Christian.

Union Quarters

This large two-story home was used to quarter Union officers during the Federal occupation in 1862.

The green-shuttered home has double galleries with an unusual column arrangement—four columns in front of six columns—and is surrounded by an attractive wrought-iron fence, all of which have withstood the Gulf storms in a grand manner. Private.

243 East Beach in Pass Christian.

Veterans of Foreign Wars Hall

The VETERANS OF FOREIGN WARS HALL dates from 1852. Mr. Charles Rhodes, mayor of the city and quartermaster of Fort Henry, was a later owner. He also dealt in general merchandise, and the structure was referred to as the Trade Palace. Private.

401 East Beach in Pass Christian.

Grass Lawn

Dr. Hiram A. G. Roberts, of Port Gibson, a landowner and surgeon, recognized the healthy climate of the Gulf Coast and erected GRASS LAWN in 1836. It is a two-story summer residence built of hand-hewn long-leaf pine with walls of cypress. Ten-foot-wide galleries originally surrounded the home at both levels, supported by two-story box columns. Wooden balustrades provided safety for the children in the family, who enjoyed the breezes from the Gulf of Mexico in this relaxing, shady place.

The interior features twenty-foot-square rooms, beautiful mantelpieces, and a walnut stairway. The home has been remodeled to accommodate extra bedrooms, baths, and closets.

GRASS LAWN, five years older than Harrison County, has housed many prominent Mississippians. Among them are Major Calvit Roberts, C.S.A., a member of the legislature; Thomas Prentiss Gary; James Dent Williams; Gulfport's first mayor, Finley B. Hewes; and John K. and Joseph W. Milner.

GRASS LAWN was restored by the Old Spanish Trail Heritage Foundation.

Open to the public Monday, Wednesday, and Friday, 10-4 and by appointment; nominal entrance fee. Call (601) 864-5019.

720 East Beach in Gulfport. 🏠

Handsboro Community

Surrounding a busy intersection on Old Pass Road in present-day Gulfport was once a sleepy little community called HANDS-BORO. The date of settlement is unknown, but in the early 1800s it was known as Buena Vista.

Before the Civil War, the largest sawmill on the coast was exporting the first lumber from this section to Europe.

The old Harry home on Tegarden Road and the Masonic Hall on Old Pass may still be seen. The women of the community met to make Confederate uniforms during the war, and after the war Jefferson Davis attended lodge meetings in the hall.

Old Pass Road in Gulfport.

Beauvoir

Facing the Gulf of Mexico among a grove of oaks, magnolias, and cedars is BEAUVOIR, the last residence of Jefferson Davis, only president of the Confederate States of America.

The white frame raised cottage, with a wide hip roof, is built in the tradition of the Southern planter of that time. As the story goes, cypress timbers were brought by camel from the swamps of Louisiana to Lake Pontchartrain and on to Biloxi by schooner.

Built in the early 1850s by James H. Brown, the main floor houses the living quarters. A broad gallery, enclosed on three sides, is approached by a graceful flight of steps with slender curved handrails. The latticed basement, with a high ceiling and well-tamped oyster-shell floor, now houses a museum containing objects related to the public life of President Davis and other historical displays.

The Dorsey family purchased the house shortly after it was constructed, and it was owned by Mrs. Sarah Ann Dorsey in 1879 when it was acquired by the Davis family. Varina Howell Davis gave it the name BEAUVOIR.

The upper story contains a main hall, double parlors, a library, and a dining room, with sleeping quarters in the back. Several small buildings are on the spacious grounds. The east cottage served as a study, and it was here that Jefferson Davis wrote *The Rise and Fall of the Confederate Government.* It now contains his books, manuscripts, and letters.

For many years after the death of Mrs. Davis, BEAUVOIR served as a home for Confederate veterans, their wives, widows, orphans, and servants.

It has now been beautifully restored by the United Daughters of the Confederacy and the Mississippi Division of the United Sons of Confederate Veterans. To the latter organization Mrs. Davis deeded the property in 1902. Its furnishings include some original pieces, the lost items being replaced by furniture of the same period.

A visit to BEAUVOIR, in its simple grandeur, takes one back in history for a moment, a time steeped in the tradition of the Old South.

Open to the public daily, 9-5; nominal entrance fee. Closed Christmas Day. Call (601) 388-1313.

200 West Beach in Biloxi. 🏠

Beauvoir

Biloxi Cemetery

Many headstones in this cemetery, known to mark the graves of many early Biloxi settlers, have had their inscriptions completely worn away by time and weather. Spanish moss protects some of the plots; others are covered by oyster shells.

The tomb of Jean Cuevas is in the older section. He was a hero of the War of 1812, who refused to show the British the waterways into New Orleans.

U.S. 90 (west of Porter Avenue) in Biloxi.

Biloxi Lighthouse

Biloxi Lighthouse

Built in 1848, the BILOXI LIGHTHOUSE stands today in an amazing state of preservation, still sending out light to seafarers. When Federal troops occupied Fort Massachusetts, a local citizen is said to have climbed the sixty-five-foot tower and removed the lens from the light and buried it; it was dug up and restored to its original place at the end of the war.

Another story tells us that this was the only public structure in the South to be draped in mourning when Abraham Lincoln was assassinated. For several weeks the usual bright white lighthouse was painted black. When John F. Kennedy was assassinated, it was again draped in mourning.

Open to the public May-Labor Day, Wednesday-Saturday, 10-6; Sunday, noon-6; nominal entrance fee. Special group arrangements may be made year-round. Call (601) 435-6294.

U.S. 90 at Porter Avenue in Biloxi. 🏛

Carriage House

The old CARRIAGE HOUSE on the old Baldwin Wood estate was badly damaged by Hurricane Camille but has been restored by the City of Biloxi. The Biloxi Art Association now uses this landmark for its gallery.

It was built in 1870 by Charles T. Howard, later owned by the Baldwin Woods.

Bellman (near U.S. 90) in Biloxi.

Church of the Redeemer

The small chapel at the rear of this property is again in use as the CHURCH OF THE REDEEMER. Built in 1853, it was attended by the Jefferson Davis family for many years.

A new, larger church, built in 1889, was destroyed by Hurricane Camille in 1969; only the bell tower remains.

At the southwest corner of the property is the famed, majestic live oak that is the subject of a fascinating Indian legend. One of the tree's branches is twisted to form a complete circle. The story tells us that the daughter of a Biloxi chief wished to marry the chief of an enemy tribe. Her father said, "My child shall never wed a brave from another tribe 'til a ring grows in yonder oak." During the night a storm twisted the large branch, and the old chief, feeling nature had surely conspired to help the young couple, gave his blessing.

U.S. 90 at Bellman in Biloxi.

Creole Cottage

Built in 1860, this quaint cottage housed the first free public library in the state of Mississippi. In 1898, Miss Mollie Rodenburg taught school in the morning and in the afternoon operated the library, where a large number of books had been donated by Biloxi citizens.

Later the little house was owned by D. Harry Schmidt, who donated it to the City of Biloxi in 1972. The cottage was moved from its original site and now sits on the lawn of the Biloxi Library and Cultural Center. Private.

Lamuese Street in Biloxi.

Fort Massachusetts

Construction began on this forbidding red brick structure in the 1850s when Jefferson Davis, then U.S. secretary of war, sent workmen to the island, twelve miles from the mainland. The fortification was used briefly by the Confederacy at the beginning of the Civil War and then occupied by Federal troops in December 1861, under the command of Major General Benjamin F. Butler. These troops continued work on the construction of the fort. Throughout the war, it was used as a base of operations to support the naval attack on New Orleans and for harassment of Confederate shipping along the coast.

Fort Massachusetts

One register bears the names of 153 Confederate soldiers who died here. In 1870 several companies of soldiers were removed, thus ending the island's history as a military post.

It is located on historic Ship Island, where d'Iberville's fleet anchored in 1699 and which remained the base for French exploration of the area. The island was also used as a British base in the War of 1812 under the command of Sir Edward Pakenham.

Excursion boats daily from Biloxi and Gulfport. Call (601) 875-0821. 🏛

Old Brick House

The Biloxi Garden Center, known for many years as OLD BRICK HOUSE, was built on land obtained by an early French settler, Jean Baptiste Carquote. Construction date of the house is unknown, but it is believed to date back to the 1830s or 1840s.

One of the early owners was John L. Henley, mayor of Biloxi during the Civil War, who retained the property until 1872. Since that time it has changed ownership several times.

138

Situated on the back bay, it measures fifty feet by thirty feet (excluding the twelve-foot gallery rebuilt after Hurricane Camille). The one-and-a-half-story common-bond brick structure features paneled doors in the three recessed front entrances.

Some consider it to be the oldest house still standing in Biloxi.

Open year-round by appointment; nominal entrance fee. Call (601) 374-0323 or 432-5836.

410 East Bayview in Biloxi. 🏠

Old French House

Dating from 1737, OLD FRENCH HOUSE is a one-and-a-half-story cottage. Rambling additions have erased much of the original design, but the iron railing and grillwork around the front porch are reminiscent of the early period.

With solid brick walls and hand-hewn cypress columns, this sturdy house has been an area landmark for many generations and is presently Mary Mahoney's Old French House Restaurant.

Opens daily at 11; closed Sunday. Call (601) 374-0163.

138 Rue Magnolia in Biloxi.

Old Magnolia Hotel

One of the oldest hostelries on the coast is the MAGNOLIA HOTEL, built in 1847. A large square frame building with wide comfortable galleries, the building has been moved to its present location and beautifully restored. It now serves as the home of the Gulf Coast Carnival Association Mardi Gras Exhibit and as a historic landmark.

Open to the public Monday, Tuesday, and Thursday, 9-noon; Wednesday and Friday, 2-5; nominal entrance fee. Call (601) 432-8806.

Rue Magnolia in Biloxi. 🏠

Old Magnolia Hotel

Poet-Priest House

This was once the home of Father Abram Joseph Ryan, known as the poet-priest of the Confederacy. He erected a cross in the front steps to identify his house. After his death, the cross was removed, and a volunteer palm tree grew up through the steps. It is now a giant tree and attracts marked attention. Private.

1428 West Beach (U.S. 90) in Biloxi.

Spanish House

A business firm now occupies the home which a Spanish army captain built, probably in the late 1700s. It is a two-story house, the only architectural remnant of the days when Biloxi was under Spanish rule, 1780-1810.

Constructed of cement over double brick, its doors and windows are deep set, and low ceilings of the rooms are supported by cypress beams. Simplicity of design uncluttered by any adornment makes the house seem austere.

206 Water (near Rue Magnolia) in Biloxi.

Tullis-Toledano Manor

This two-and-a-half-story house, constructed entirely of local brick, was built in 1856 by Christoval and Mathilde Toledano. Toledano, a prominent New Orleans cotton broker, built the manor as a summer residence and second home.

The house remained in the family until 1886. It went through a succession of owners before the estate was reunited under Garner and Mary Lee Tullis in 1939.

TULLIS-TOLEDANO MANOR was severely damaged by Hurricane Camille in 1969. In 1975 the house was purchased and restored by the City of Biloxi. Although maintained as a period house, the manor also serves as a center of community activity and is often used for weddings, parties, and receptions.

Open to the public Monday-Friday, 10-noon, 1-5. Call (601) 435-6294.

360 Beach Boulevard in Biloxi.

Ralph Wood House

This antebellum home, in a beautiful setting facing the Gulf of Mexico, dates from 1852. Its two stories are a brick basement with a second level of wood, which was typical of the architecture of that period. The broad veranda is approached by a double stairway. Private.

523 East Beach Boulevard in Biloxi.

Woodlawn

This typical Southern colonial two-story brick home was heavily damaged by Hurricane Camille but still proudly stands facing the Gulf of Mexico in a beautiful setting of giant live oak trees.

WOODLAWN, sometimes called the old Philbrick house, dates from earlier than 1763. The original plan included outside stairways and battened shutters to avoid the tax that the French levied on inside stairways and latticed shutters. Another feature was the recessed doorway with an exquisite fanlight transom and sidelights. Private.

947 East Beach in Biloxi.

Austin Home

Of typical Southern architecture, with the veranda across the entire front, is the AUSTIN HOME. It is a duplicate of a house, destroyed by fire, that was built in 1840 on the same site.

Unusual features of this place are a moat and floors of bird's-eye maple. Private.

545 Front Beach in Ocean Springs.

Bel Vue

The oldest home in Ocean Springs is the one-and-a-half-story Davidson residence, BEL VUE, built in 1827. In a lovely garden setting, it follows the typical West Indian colonial style of architecture. Private.

810 Iberville in Ocean Springs.

Brooks Home

One of the most interesting homes in Ocean Springs, both architecturally and historically, is the Fred Brooks residence. It was built in 1881 by August Von Rosenbeau, a prominent civic leader and businessman.

For twenty-five years, Charlie Dryden, famed New York *Tribune* sports writer, wintered in this home.

The quaint gingerbread-balconied upstairs porch is of special interest. Private.

910 Calhoun in Ocean Springs.

Cassanova Home

This attractive Southern cottage, which dates from the 1870s, is a one-story structure built of handmade bricks. Of note are the intricate, well-detailed posts on the front porch. Private.

900 Robinson in Ocean Springs.

Cedar Hill

CEDAR HILL once served as the original Ocean Springs post office and as a rooming house for steamship passengers arriving at the foot of Jackson Avenue.

It is designed along the lines of the typical summer beach home, with wide eaves and built high off the ground. Private.

315 Jackson Avenue in Ocean Springs.

Fort Maurepas Site

The site of FORT MAUREPAS is historically important. It was here, in 1699, that Pierre LeMoyne Sieur d'Iberville established the stronghold at "Old Biloxey," present-day Ocean Springs. It was the first French settlement and the first capital of the Louisiana colony.

A marker may be seen where the cornerstone was found; however, there is considerable evidence that the fort was located along the high bluffs by Lovers Lane.

Front Beach in Ocean Springs.

Garrard Home

Shaded by century-old live oak trees, this one-story comfortable frame dwelling, which dates from the 1880s, features the popular dogtrot in the rear. Private.

1119 Iberville in Ocean Springs.

Howell Home

One of the oldest and most carefully preserved homes in the city is this one-and-a-half-story dormered cottage with an attractive and comfortable front porch. It dates from about 1842. Private.

214 Washington in Ocean Springs.

Love Home

The Travis LOVE HOME, completed in 1890, is of Victorian design. Architectural features include the stained-glass windows and elaborate columns. Private.

406 Jackson in Ocean Springs.

Old Louisville and Nashville Depot

This railroad station, which once played such an important role in the growth and development of Ocean Springs, now serves as the Chamber of Commerce headquarters.

It is of Victorian architecture and was built in 1903.

1000 Washington Avenue in Ocean Springs.

Palfrey Home

One of the oldest homes in Ocean Springs is the Palfrey residence. It is typical of the summer homes built for comfort and spaciousness, with the usual broad front veranda to catch the Gulf breezes.

The sloping roof is interrupted by a large, two-window dormer arrangement over the front entrance. Private.

Lovers Lane in Ocean Springs.

Patterson Home

One of the finest examples of Southern architecture is the one-and-a-half-story two-dormered PATTERSON HOME. Completed in 1880, it is of frame construction, well proportioned, and in excellent condition. Private.

527 Cleveland in Ocean Springs.

St. John's Episcopal Church

The history of this beautiful church spans at least one century, although the records have been lost. The building, constructed between 1891 and 1892 of native yellow long-leaf pine, is reputed to have been designed by Louis Sullivan, the noted Chicago architect who wintered in Ocean Springs.

The church features beautiful stained-glass windows. The bell, made from 492 Mexican silver dollars, was added in 1903. Private.

711 Porter in Ocean Springs.

Saxon Home

This multigabled, two-story house was built in the 1880s with many manifestations of the Victorian period. It has been carefully preserved and adds to the beauty and charm of Jackson Avenue. Private.

318 Jackson in Ocean Springs.

Schmidt Home

This old place, which dates from 1840, is a one-story cottage. One of the oldest homes in the city, its primitive lines attest to its age. Private.

505 Jackson in Ocean Springs.

Shearwater Pottery

The visitor winds through deep woods to one of the most interesting landmarks of the area, the SHEARWATER POTTERY location. The oldest building in the complex, built in 1830, was originally a farmhouse. The pottery shop was established in 1928.

One of the structures is a rammed-earth house; another is decorated with a mural by the artist Walter Anderson, whose family still own and operate the pottery business.

Showroom open to the public Monday-Saturday, 9-5:30; Sunday, 1-5:30. Walter Anderson Cottage open Thursday, 1-4, or by appointment. Workshop open Monday-Friday, 9-4. Call (601) 875-7320.

South on Pershing to 102 Shearwater Drive in Ocean Springs.

Louis Sullivan Home

This was once the summer home of Louis Sullivan, a teacher of Frank Lloyd Wright and considered by many to be the father of American architecture.

A one-story shingle residence built in 1890, it has had several structural changes since that time. Private.

South on Pershing Avenue to Shearwater Drive and East Beach Drive in Ocean Springs.

Watson Home

This Italianate home was built in 1873. Ancient oak trees enhance its beauty.

The furnishings include priceless Louis XV antiques and beautiful appointments, including a rare eighteenth-century French chandelier. Private.

505 Front Beach in Ocean Springs.

Widmer Home

Tucked behind a picket fence, this quaint one-story frame New Orleans cottage was completed about 1840. It is the only residence in Ocean Springs of this particular architectural design. Private.

520 Jackson in Ocean Springs.

Winklejohn Home

Another of Ocean Springs' several sturdy antebellum homes is the WINKLEJOHN HOME, a one-story cottage built between 1840 and 1850.

The architecture is typical of the period, with columns of the large veranda supporting the sloping two-dormered roof. Private.

418 Martin in Ocean Springs.

Gautier Plantation

A broad gallery completely surrounds this beautiful French cottage built in 1856 by Fernando Gautier, an early settler. It has remained in the family and contains the original furnishings.

Many doors and windows allow breezes to flow throughout this house, giving a glimpse into a bygone era.

The dining room and kitchen, separated from the main house, contain many unusual utensils and a massive fireplace, interesting samples of early Americana. Private.

In Gautier.

Gautier Plantation

Oldfields

Built in 1849 by Alfred Lewis, OLDFIELDS is similar in design to the Briars in Natchez, with windows across the front opening onto the veranda. There are four dormered windows at the second level. High ceilings and huge rooms around the broad hall make this antebellum residence spacious and comfortable.

The story is told that during the Federal occupation of the home during the Civil War, Mrs. Lewis and her children were imprisoned overnight in the attic. The next morning, she walked past the guard, entered the dining room where the officers were enjoying breakfast, and stated, "This is my home, and you are eating my food while my children go hungry." The men gallantly rose and served the family a delicious breakfast.

In 1904 the plantation was acquired by W. W. Grinstead, whose daughters married the Anderson brothers, owners of Shearwater Pottery in Ocean Springs. Private.

Near Gautier.

Denny Home

It is believed that the DENNY HOME is one of the oldest in Jackson County. It is a raised frame planter-type cottage with double entrance doors and tall windows opening onto the front veranda.

The magnificent tree, "Lovers Oak," is located nearby. According to legend, young Pascagoula braves serenaded the Indian maidens on summer nights, and the Pascagoula River, listening, began to sing; it is one of the many stories about the singing river. Private.

Front Street, on the river, off Dupont Avenue in Pascagoula.

Fredric House

The original back portion of this old place dates from before the Civil War. Set among gnarled live oaks, it must have been a showplace in its time. Private.

At the foot of Delmas Avenue, on the river, in Pascagoula.

Longfellow House

Sometimes known as Bellevue or the Pollock place, LONGFELLOW HOUSE was built in 1854.

Constructed of wood and stone, its one-and-a-half stories, above a raised brick basement, are approached by double winding stairways, which have intricate iron grillwork handrails.

While visiting Bellevue, Henry Wadsworth Longfellow was inspired to write "The Building of the Ship," the poem that refers to Pascagoula's sunny bay.

This beautifully restored home is now owned by Ingalls Shipyards. Private.

East Beach in Pascagoula.

Old Spanish Fort

Louisville and Nashville Depot

The railroad had an impact on Pascagoula, not only in the development of industry but in the increasing number of tourists who came to enjoy the balmy Gulf breezes at this seaside resort.

A small, one-story rectangular frame structure, the depot is topped by a three-section slated hip roof that is accented with dormers and gables. The building's appearance has not been substantially changed since it was constructed in 1904. Private.

Railroad Avenue in Pascagoula. 🏛

Old Spanish Fort

Built in 1718, OLD SPANISH FORT is reputed to be the oldest structure in the Mississippi Valley.

The original owner, Sieur Joseph de la Pointe, who never used the building as a military post, had in mind a well-fortified residence when he constructed a house with outside walls measuring fifteen to thirty inches in thickness.

A German immigrant, Von Krebs, married the daughter of de la Pointe, and for many years the place was called Krebs' Fort.

Primitive in architectural design, the low, cottagelike farmhouse has had little remodeling over the past two and a half centuries. The original cypress timbered walls, floors, and ceiling are intact.

Now a museum displaying historic memorabilia of the area, it is owned by the Jackson County Historical Society.

Open to the public daily, except Thursday. November-March, 10-4; April-October, 10-4:30; nominal entrance fee. Call (601) 769-1505.

North on Magnolia from U.S. 90; turn left on Morgan Avenue to 4602 Fort Drive in Pascagoula.

Fairley House

This old home, which dates from 1836, commands a magnificent view of Krebs' Lake and the Pascagoula rivers. Once part of a vast estate, the house has changed little since its construction. Private.

River Road in Moss Point.

Griffin House

Dr. Erasmus Franklin Griffin, prominent educator and civic leader, built this home for his bride, Julia Russ, in the early 1860s, at the confluence of the Escatawpa and Pascagoula rivers. It is at the site where Moss Point (sometimes called Mossey Point by loggers) was given its name. An eight-foot granite slab has been erected to commemorate the event. Nearby is Old Spanish Trail, originally a Choctaw Indian trade route.

All of the lumber used in the construction of the one-story raised cottage is virgin long-leaf yellow pine. The roof is shaped in the early pyramidal design. A front gallery is supported by four heart-pine pillars approximately sixteen inches square. The banisters are handmade, and handmade bricks support the foundation.

The house served for many years as the office of the L. N. Dantzler Lumber Company. The approach to this landmark is through a spectacular live oak grove planted many years before the Civil War. Private.

101 Griffin Street (River Road) at the Escatawpa River in Moss Point.

Meridian Area

Introduction

In 1864, four years after the founding of Meridian, Union General Sherman destroyed the city and stated in his report, "Meridian no longer exists." Today it is a thriving metropolis with several historical attractions in the area.

Grand Opera House

Mention must be made of the historic building which is now occupied by a modern store in downtown Meridian. Having housed the GRAND OPERA HOUSE of Meridian at the turn of the century, it was considered by many to be the finest in the South.

The building was converted in 1919 into a movie theater and in 1926 was closed. Today, totally divested of its former splendor, just a shell of the building is visible to remind the visitor of the grand manner of cultural entertainment of the past.

2208 Fifth Street in Meridian. 🏛

Merrehope

Richard McLemore, first settler of Meridian, gave the property on which MERREHOPE is situated to his daughter, Juriah, in 1859. She and her husband, W. H. Jackson, built a small cottage believed to have been incorporated into the existing twenty-room mansion.

A succession of owners followed and in 1904 the home was purchased by S. H. Floyd, who remodeled it extensively. This imposing mansion was divided into apartments from 1914 until 1968, when a group of women's clubs formed the Meridian Restorations Foundation, Inc. and acquired the home. It was named MERREHOPE for the city of Meridian with "hope" that it could be restored to its former grandeur. This task was accomplished with the help of numerous government agencies and private organizations.

The exterior is designed with nine fluted Ionic columns, bracketed eaves, a graceful bay rising to the second level, a large railed balcony, and a beautiful doorway featuring etched ruby-colored glass in the sidelights and transom. Cast-iron mantelpieces, marble hearths, plaster cornices, and ceiling medallions are included in the interior.

During the month of December, the rooms are filled with elaborately decorated Christmas trees with varying themes which attract widespread attention.

Open to the public year-round, Monday-Saturday, 9-5; Sunday, 1-5; nominal entrance fee. Call (601) 483-8439.

905 Martin Luther King, Jr. Memorial Drive in Meridian. 🏛

Merrehope

Jimmie Rodgers Memorial Museum

In Highland Park may be seen a memorial to Jimmie Rodgers, a native of Meridian considered by many to be the grandfather of today's country music.

The monument is inscribed to "America's Blue Yodeler—immortal ballad singing brakeman—whose great talents are preserved on RCA Victor Records." Museum exhibits include Rodgers' guitar, personal items, concert clothing, sheet music, and correspondence.

Open to the public Monday-Saturday, 10-4; Sunday, 1-5. Closed January 1, Thanksgiving, and Christmas; nominal entrance fee. Call (601) 485-1808.

In Highland Park (north on Forty-fifth Street to State Boulevard) in Meridian.

Frank W. Williams House

Built by Frank W. Williams in about 1886, this Victorian house stands as a lasting tribute to one of Meridian's outstanding citizens. Mr. Williams was instrumental in the development of the insurance industry in Mississippi. This two-story house remained in the family until it was given to the Meridian Restorations Foundation. It was moved to its present location in 1978, and has been completely restored.

Open to the public Monday-Saturday, 9-5; Sunday, 1-5; nominal entrance fee. Closes at 4 during the winter months. Call (601) 483-8439.

Next door to MERREHOPE at 905 Martin Luther King, Jr. Memorial Drive in Meridian.

Sam Dale Memorial

Born in 1772 Sam Dale, an Indian scout and hero of the War of 1812, rode from Georgia to the Battle of New Orleans with news for General Andrew Jackson.

A memorial park and statue have been dedicated to this brave man. The visitor may view bas-reliefs depicting the outstanding events of this pioneer's life. Dale died in 1841 at the age of sixty-nine.

On Mississippi 39 in Daleville.

Boler Inn

BOLER INN is situated in the small community of Union. It was established around 1833-34 and was the scene of Civil War battles.

The inn was a haven for many weary visitors who traveled the old stage line between Montgomery, Alabama, and Jackson, Mississippi. Although the railroad displaced the use of the stagecoach, this historic old hotel is still well preserved. A historical marker may be seen on the front lawn.

In Union.

Index